Cardinal Spellman has given the rights to this book to the New York Foundling Hospital, which cares for children without distinction of race, creed or color.

THE FOUNDLING

The Foundling

by FRANCIS CARDINAL SPELLMAN

New York
CHARLES SCRIBNER'S SONS

COPYRIGHT, 1951, BY
CHARLES SCRIBNER'S SONS

Copyright, 1951, by
Hearst Magazines, Inc.

Printed in the United States of America

All rights reserved. No part of this book may be reproduced in any form without the permission of Charles Scribner's Sons

TO THE MULTITUDE OF PASSERS-BY
AND THE MANY OF EVERY CREED
WHO ENTER ST. PATRICK'S OPEN DOORS
THEREIN QUIETLY TO PRAY
HUMBLY I DEDICATE THIS BOOK
WITH MY HEART'S HOPE THAT ALL MAY BE
INSPIRED BETTER TO LOVE AND SERVE GOD
AND RESPECT ONE ANOTHER IN THE
GLORIOUS COMMON CAUSE OF
LIBERTY AND JUSTICE AND PEACE
FOR ALL MANKIND

THE FOUNDLING

PART 1

Chapter 1

NO ONE noticed the solitary, wistful soldier peeling an orange with his teeth. Once this lean, long-legged lad could have taken the fruit in his hands and stripped its skin with his fingers. But that was in other years—years before war screamed into the world, mastered men, bent them to its vengeful, lustful will and left them, as it had left Paul, struck down and maimed in the Argonne.

All day long Paul Taggart had tramped the East River waterfront. It was a familiar place. Often he had roamed through the markets and around the coal yards. It was good to sit on a sun-warmed pier and watch the tugs chugging north and south. The shouting of the vendors, the oily odor of fish lately hustled out of Sheepshead Bay and points off New England, the longshoremen sprawling in the shade, the clatter of the oystermen's knives prying open the tight shells of the blue points, the coal scoop, with iron mouth agape, dropping on lithe steel cables into a barge and coming up with a dripping jawful of coke—all this wondrous waterfront life had never before failed to soothe him.

But now, he only felt the night, cold, black, and desolate. Paul looked back at the great city—once *his* city—with its cluster of buildings silhouetted against the hills of heaven, their thousand tiny, friendly lights signaling like mothers' lamps on window sills. For seventeen months of anguish he had dreamed of this night. Yes, he was home at last, but tonight none of these shimmering lights beckoned to befriend him.

Paul shivered. Suddenly he was no longer hungry. He was remembering the words the nurse had spoken to him that terrible morning in France, "Thank God, soldier, you're alive." Her voice was gentle and Paul thought he saw pity sweep swiftly across her face. But it was only when he had tried to brush the pain from his own face with his right hand that Paul Taggart translated into its real meaning the compassion he read in the nurse's eyes. And because he had never cried in the face of a woman, he looked quickly away.

"My arm . . ." he began, but his voice choked in his throat.

Five weeks later, when the doctor removed the bandages from his face and allowed him to look into a mirror, there had come the new awakening. In the instant when he first saw his face, Paul closed his eyes. Then he walked blindly back to bed with the memory of that scar burning into his tormented brain more deeply than the wound itself cut into his torn and aching flesh.

That had been six weeks ago.

Tonight Paul's fingers traced the jagged, livid line, ending suddenly below his left eye, that seemed to cut apart one half of his face. And because he was young and wanted to be with those he loved, Paul felt lonely and afraid.

"It's going to be tough facing them all," he whispered to the night, "plenty tough." Behind him he knew the city held enveloped in its arms, awaiting his return, old friends, his mother, and closest to his heart—Ellen.

But out there, in the murky half-light, floating mid sky and river, Paul saw Tim, Jack, Sam, Gordon, Ken, his buddies who, with millions unknown to him, had fought to make the world safe for democracy. Five soldiers, all from different parts of one blessed land, boys of different beliefs, but all bearing one bond of selfless love for one another as they fought, lived and died to bring liberty and peace to the oppressed and lowly of the earth.

He remembered big Jack—only twenty-one, gay, handsome, laughing—reading aloud his letters from home, his even, strong teeth gleaming white against the natural tan of his skin. Jack shared his fun, his gifts, his rations as he shared his life—to bring joy to others less joyous than himself. And then Jack lay a heap of raw agony upon his stretcher, his strong legs and chest smashed beyond repair, even then with death within him, trying to smile at Sam lying there beside him.

Smilin' Sam had stood sentry all through that Christmas eve of 1917—so Tim could go to church. Sam might be whole and safe now, if he had lived his short life-span loving others less. "You go, Tim," he had said, "It's His birthday. Didn't He always say men must share and live in love as brothers? Go, Tim, and pray a prayer for me!" Was not this charity more truly Christlike than that of many who *called* themselves Christian?

Short weeks later Sam's body lay singed and crushed and streaked with blood, but his spirit lived on to seed kinship among men.

The twins, Gordon and Ken, died together as they had lived and fought together. The firm, sturdy hand of Ken had been twined in the blond hair of his brother to give solace and strength; his outstretched hand bearing witness to unfaltering love and loyalty, as together they entered the deep valley of death on the road to eternal life.

And Tim—Tim died as he prayed to die—with the name of God upon his lips and grace in his heart. After seventy-two hours of reconnaissance, dead tired before turning in at 4 A.M., he had nonetheless sought out the chaplain and received Communion. Then he, too, was gone. His young body and brain had served his country well; his soul served God and journeyed to Heaven.

"Thank God you're alive," the nurse had said to Paul, for nearly his whole company had been wiped out, and of the six friends, he alone was left.

Paul stood up suddenly and shook himself as if to be free of the fetters of memory. Shielding his scarred face from the biting wind, he walked slowly away from the melancholy river. He walked as if a hidden hand were gently guiding him away from the black, cold, churning waterfront which had stirred within him shocking, sickening, rebellious thoughts born of loneliness, futility, and despair.

Just how he reached the Cathedral that night, Paul never knew. But there he was, moving haltingly down the aisle, shyly conscious of rows of bended heads and kneeling figures that formed deep, silent human valleys on either side of him. Poinsettias and holly, reminders of Christmas, pressed into his memory and awakened him to time and reality. It was, he then remembered, the twenty-eighth of December—the very day he had always hoped to return home—to surprise Ellen. It was her birthday. He'd surprise her tonight, all right, he mused, surprise and shock her with his empty sleeve and garish, clownish face. But tonight, though he longed for his sweetheart and his mother, he couldn't bear to return home. He didn't want to see anyone he knew. He didn't want anyone he knew to *see him!*

Yet here the slow, steady stream of people circling the high altar, the hundreds of tiny flames from lighted vigils, the glorious hues from the ceiling chandeliers spilling in cascades of light upon the bowed heads, all these warmed and comforted him.

Paul wanted to follow the quiet throngs and find what sped them on their way. But suddenly he felt lax and tired. In deference to the beauty and reverence around him, Paul knelt and bent his close-cropped head in pleading prayer. "Oh God, strengthen me—and give me peace!"

Peace! The word upon his lips shocked him. Again memories lashed out like wild, whirling waterfalls, flooding and threatening to submerge him in despair. Mercifully, only for a moment, for Paul Taggart sank into a corner of the pew and fell asleep—God's grant of grace to the first prayer Paul Taggart, the man, had ever prayed!

He didn't know how long he had slept, but when he waked, he was alone. The dying yellow candle flames threw dancing figures against the high stone walls, and once again Paul felt himself strangely drawn to the back of the Cathedral. That blue glow of a lamp! What was it there behind the high altar? And then beneath the rough "rocks" of a canvas cave, Paul discovered the magnet that had attracted myriads of devoted people to the shrine.

"Christmas crib," he breathed.

He sank slowly to his knees and began to identify the figures clustered in the straw. The baby, of course, was Jesus. The woman in blue and white was Mary, His Mother. And there behind the sheep and oxen . . .

Paul was startled. He closed his eyes, then looked again. For a second he thought he saw a tiny fist raised above the straw. It must be imagination. Strange things happen to a wounded soldier just home from war, dozing alone in a lofty Cathedral. Hadn't he, only a few hours ago, seen before him on the river the faces of his friends—long dead upon battlefronts beyond the tumbling waters of the sea? Miracles didn't happen in 1918. His mood, his capricious memory would have no truck with anything like that. And then Paul heard the sound, the soft unmistakable whimpering of a baby.

He jumped to his feet and hurried to the nearest door.

Things like that scared one. Miracles were all right in their place, but on a night like tonight . . .

Suddenly a sharp, pitiful wail pierced the Cathedral, and pierced, too, his lonely heart. Paul stopped. The fretful crying continued. Timorously, he retraced his steps, leaned over the rail and looked deep into the crib.

"Good Lord, is it . . . it is *You*?" he asked hoarsely. A squall of infant indignation answered him.

Then he saw it in the far corner of the crib, nestled deep in the folds of a brown blanket. It was a baby, all right. Living, breathing, kicking, but mostly crying. Paul looked around him. Not a soul astir. Clumsily he climbed over the rail.

"All right," he whispered, lifting and juggling the baby at a precarious angle. "All right. Don't cry. I'll fix you up." His anxious voice belied his brave words.

Back on the other side of the rail, Paul sat down in the nearest pew and studied this unusual bundle. Eyes, ears, nose, mouth, brown curly hair—it bore a striking resemblance to all the babies he had ever seen.

"Stop crying, baby," Paul said, bouncing it on his knee. And, surprisingly, the baby stopped.

Paul laughed softly. For the first time since that terrible day when he had looked upon himself, fear-frozen, in the hospital mirror in France, he sensed a feeling akin to joy. For he was exercising a privilege he thought forever lost to him—the man-privilege of drawing someone close within the circle of his arm and protecting her. Or was it him?

Paul still smiling at himself and at his baby, put on his

The Foundling

cap, draped the empty right sleeve of his coat over the infant, rose and walked quietly past the statues standing guard in their niches of the Church. As usual, they were holding their rigid vigil in the south transept. Saint Patrick stood in his six-bayed, lustreless window at Fiftieth Street. The gentle Apostle John, with book and poised pen, looked fixedly past the Palisades toward the north. Only the Pieta, dream of Michelangelo, seemed alive. The glimmering candles cast soft shadows like caressing, compassionate fingertips upon the Sorrowful Mother holding within her arms the lifeless body of her Son. She had *two* loving arms, but they held against her blessed breast a crucified Christ!

The soldier holding his sleeping baby tightly pressed against his heart felt grief for her and joy for himself and whispered reassuringly as he passed:

"I'll take care of *this* baby for you, Mary."

Outside the snow was falling steadily, gently touching each late passerby. Paul hastily hailed a cab at Fiftieth Street, clambered in awkwardly and sat huddled in a corner. Lucky the driver still felt the Christmas kindness toward uniforms, Paul thought, as he glanced at the bundle nestled in the crook of his good arm.

"Where to?"

"Better drive through the park," Paul answered quickly.

"The park?" Indignantly the man turned to glare at his passenger. In the darkness he failed to see the baby.

"Just drive slowly. I'll tell you where to go later."

"Just as you say, buddy. Just as you say," the driver mumbled. Wiping a blob of snow from the windshield and muffling himself to the ears, he began the easy business of driving in a trafficless New York.

Paul settled back and arranged the dangling sleeve of his coat snugly around the baby. The first exciting moments of his discovery were wearing off and now the problem of what he should do with the child was becoming acute.

Abandoned babies were, to be sure, nothing new in a city like New York. The papers frequently carried stories about children left in doorways, stations and churches. He had usually dismissed them with a "poor kid" or "tough luck."

But now that he had a real, live baby on his lap, the situation became startlingly important and personal. An abanboned baby was much more than a picture in a newspaper or a tightly phrased news account. This one was a breathing, warm, human bundle with a jaunty little wool helmet that kept slipping over its eyes and, dangling from strings, two mittens that were so tiny they made him laugh deep inside.

"I guess you're glad to be back from the war," the driver's voice interrupted Paul's thoughts.

Yes, he was glad to be back. A sudden jounce in a rut lifted Paul out of the seat. The baby began to whimper.

The driver cocked his ear. "You know," he said in a voice touched lightly with wonderment, "you know, I could've sworn I heard a baby just then."

"You did," Paul said, simply. "I got a baby right here on my lap."

"What!" the driver gulped.

The Foundling

"Found him about half a hour ago."

"Found him!" the driver exploded, jamming on his brakes. "You mean you actually found a baby!" Suddenly he spied the bundle under the soldier's sleeve. "Holy smokes, soldier! That's against the law. I mean, you can't just pick up babies and . . ." A fresh squall from the baby interrupted him. "What are you going to do with him?"

"I don't know," Paul said.

The driver scratched the stubble on his chin. "Where did you find him?" he managed at last.

Paul told him the story. The cabby listened with growing consternation.

"If you take my advice, you'll get rid of that baby fast, soldier. For all you know that kid might've been kidnapped."

"The baby's only an orphan," Paul said stubbornly.

"Orphan or no orphan, a cab ain't a place for a baby on a night like this. You'd better take him to a police station."

"Nothing doing," Paul snapped. He had to raise his voice to make himself heard above the baby's crying.

"Well, what are you going to do?" the driver asked, heatedly. "Ride around all night?"

"I'd like to keep him."

"It's against the law. The first thing you know, we'll both be locked up," the man bellowed.

"You just keep driving and stop yelling," Paul shouted. "You're scaring the life out of this baby."

The cab groaned into motion amidst the muttering of the cabby, the threatening of the soldier, and the wailing of the baby.

The Foundling

"Listen, buddy," the driver cajoled when the cab finally turned out of the 110th Street exit, "you might as well make up your mind that this thing can't go on forever. Why don't you be reasonable and put the baby in a nice place where someone can take good care of it?"

Paul stared glumly out of the window of the cab. The driver was right, of course.

"Where do they bring lost babies?" he asked, finally. "Where's a real good place to bring a lost baby?"

The cabby scratched his chin, "There's a place on Sixty-Eighth Street takes care of them. Foundling Hospital. We drivers know about it. It's okay. Some kind of Sisters run it."

"Sisters?"

"Yeah."

They were moving directly east, now, and the streets were completely covered with snow.

"I might never see him again, if I leave him there," Paul said.

"What's the difference?" the driver asked. "Once you get rid of the kid, your worries are over."

Paul took a deep breath and looked at the baby. The small face was relaxed in sleep again. Gently he freed his left arm and ran his fingers lightly over the child's features. Softly he spoke to the baby. "It's as if you were my own little kid. You're just the kind of kid I've always wanted." He was ashamed then that his eyes were wet. And yet he was not really ashamed. "You might have been Ellen's baby . . . and mine," he finished, as he bent more closely to the child.

The Foundling

"Well, what do you want to do?" the driver repeated, impatiently.

"I guess you'd better drive to that Foundling place," Paul said.

The cab rolled slowly through the storm. And while the snow was falling, a city dreamed, a cabby smiled, and a baby slept in the strong cradle of a soldier's left arm.

Chapter 2

SISTER MARGARET MARY of the New York Foundling Hospital was sitting in her wicker chair. The night-light, burning dimly behind her, flung her shadow down the dormitory and across the cribs. Twenty-seven orphan babies were obligingly asleep at that magic hour in the early morning. So Sister Margaret relaxed. The clock chimed the quarter hour.

"A quarter past two," Sister Margaret whispered.

She closed her eyes and listened to the wind fluting a wild song of winter over the sill. She shivered and pulled the shawl about her shoulders. Only twenty-four years old, Sister Margaret did what most young nuns do, sooner or later. She was thinking about herself; thinking about this life she had chosen one bright day in August. And she was thinking, particularly, about the telephone call.

The sad, bright, poignant events of the past five years

The Foundling

shifted in the kaleidoscope of her memory. She remembered that last night at home when her brother Joey stole into the room and helped her pack the trunk. She remembered how neatly everything had been arranged: the black merino wool for her shawl, the albatross for caps and habit, broadcloth and sateen, prayer books and thimble, soap (unscented), and high black shoes.

"The trunk's packed," Joey had announced, triumphantly to the family gathered in the kitchen. "The trunk's packed and Peg's all set to go."

Her father had looked up at her and smiled over the edge of his newspaper. But her mother, sitting beside the kitchen table, did not lift her head.

"You'll be able to come to see me often," she said. "It's not as if I were going to the foreign missions," she added, trying to brighten the dark silence that had settled suddenly over the room. And her mother bravely smiled through tears as in fond embrace she blessed and said farewell to this mere child, her only daughter.

Sister Margaret Mary remembered then these last two years at the Foundling on East Sixty-Eighth Street. She remembered how she had walked timorously into the rambling red brick structure for her first interview. She remembered the long cool corridors, the soft footfalls of nurses and sisters carrying infants, the yellow faces, the white faces, the black faces of the babies, the playrooms with the little, painted chairs and the toys and, dear to her feminine heart, the fact that the children were not dressed alike as in an institution (as she had feared), but that each child seemed to wear its own suit or dress in its own becoming color—its very own. She had been shown the medical offices and the diet kitchens (two hundred and seventy baby formulas) and she had been given the assignment. It was her very first and she had accepted it with all the enthusiasm of a novice.

Her mother had been able to visit her often. Her brother, Joey, too. Sad-heartedly she recalled the last time he had come to see her—the day before he left for the Army.

"Gosh, you look nice in that outfit, Peg," he had said.

"Think so?" she smiled. And forgetting the points of her night meditation, she yielded to instinct and arranged her cap at a prim angle. She wasn't being vain about it, she hoped. It was merely a question of looking presentable; and to quiet her conscience, she recalled what the Mistress of Novices had said. "The day of the untidy saint is past." That's what Sister Agnita said, and Sister Agnita was a fastidious religious.

Gaily she and Joey walked to the gate, that last day. At the corner he turned and waved. Then, heavy-footed and sad-hearted, Sister Margaret Mary retraced her way to the house.

"God, bring Joey back safe and soon," she cried in the chapel that evening.

Sister Margaret stirred in the wicker chair. The telephone seemed to be ringing again in her ears. She recalled it clearly. Even before she lifted the receiver that night, a month ago, she knew it was her mother.

"It's bad news, Peg," her mother said. "It's Joey . . . he's been killed in France." Then her voice broke. Sister

The Foundling

Margaret tried to sound brave, to instill courage in her mother. She wanted to run to her, to comfort and sustain her. But that wasn't possible. Instead, she hurried to the chapel. Kneeling in solitude, the shadows playing upon her bowed head pressed against the hard oak of the bench, she released in prayer the flood-gates of her grief. "Dear Christ, keep my little brother Joey," she sobbed over and over again.

Sister Margaret fumbled in her habit and brought from its deep folds a picture of Joey. He had sent it to her just before leaving for France. She looked long and lovingly into the friendly, smiling eyes of her brother, and the pain that tore at her heart gathered too in her throat. Tired, chilled, and lonely, she half-dreamed again. If only she could go back home and sit in the kitchen these December afternoons; talk to her mother about the price of dry-goods and groceries at Sanderson's, about Mrs. Norton's twins, about the Burke's new automobile and a thousand and one intimate other homely joys, then perhaps the sharp-edged ache for Joey would ease into the far corners of her memory.

Suddenly, the routine of her life in the orphanage—early rising, meditation, prayers, Mass, dormitory duty—seemed unattractive. So it was to this she had dedicated her life—working from dawn to dusk, keeping vigils throughout the restless, endless night. This is what she might be asked to do the rest of her life. "O God!" she whispered, in accents she had never used before.

It would not be too unusual if she went home. Sisters left the convent, at times, for a number of different reasons. And

Sister Margaret had not even taken final vows! It would be a very simple matter to see Mother Superior, and tell her that she felt her mother needed her.

Sister Margaret's shoulders convulsed.

"Jesus, forgive me . . . I didn't mean it," she whispered. "Really, I didn't mean it."

Sister Margaret straightened her shoulders and unconsciously clenched her fists in firm resolution.

She was reaching for her chart when the doorbell rang. A swirl of snow flew in her face as she opened the door. For a moment she was blinded.

"Do you take babies here?" a voice asked.

"Come in, please," Sister Margaret invited.

"My name's Paul Taggart, I found this baby in church," the soldier began bluntly, scraping the snow off his shoes.

"Come in—come this way, please."

Sister Margaret led Paul down the corridor to the office and lighted the gas mantle. "Please sit down, sir."

Balancing the baby awkwardly, the young soldier sat in the chair. Then the Sister saw the empty sleeve. She sped across the room.

"Oh, excuse me, sir. I didn't realize . . . I'll take the baby."

To relieve the embarrassment of the soldier, as he removed his cap and stood staring down at the baby now resting in the soft folds of the nun's lap, Sister Margaret inspected the infant.

"You'll find him a mighty nice baby," Paul said. Somehow, he had decided, it had to be a him.

The Foundling

Sister Margaret smiled.

"I found him in the cathedral a couple of hours ago, and I figured this is the best place for him."

"It was kind of you to bring him."

Paul shifted uneasily.

"This is the seventh baby left in a church this year," Sister Margaret began, still trying to put the soldier at ease. Yet Paul knew her eyes had found the ugly scar on his face.

"By the way, Sister, would it be possible for me to make a claim on this baby?"

"A claim, sir?"

"Yes, a sort of an adoption claim."

"You mean you want to adopt this baby?"

"Yes."

Sister Margaret hesitated. "I couldn't give you any answer right now, tonight that is. But I'm sure Sister Superior would be only too glad to consider it. There are definite regulations we must follow, you know, and first of all we must do everything we can to try and find the baby's parents."

"I see."

"Are you married, Mr. Taggart?"

"No, Sister," Paul answered. "Do you have to be married?"

"Well—yes. Ordinarily."

"I see." Paul fumbled with the peak of his cap.

"Before we place babies for adoption, we must have assurance that they will be provided with the proper home atmosphere," Sister Margaret continued, in the routine recital of the legalistic formula.

"I understand," Paul said, helplessly.

"In other words, a baby ought to have a mother," Sister Margaret said, forcing a smile. "Best of all, it ought to have its *own* mother."

Paul cleared his throat. "Well, I guess I'd better be going," he said, rising.

"I'd like your name and address, sir, if you don't mind," Sister Margaret said.

Paul held the baby while she noted these and the scant details he could give her about the infant. As he returned the child to the nun's arms, he said, "I suppose this will be the last time I'll ever see him."

"Oh, no! You may visit him any time you wish."

Paul brightened at that and reached over to stroke the face of the sleeping baby.

Sister Margaret studied the soldier's features. It would have been a handsome face if that scar did not strike the eye so forcibly. And because of the mute melancholy written there, she found herself saying, "I hope that you will come back some day and adopt the baby, Mr. Taggart. That is, if we can't reach the parents."

The soldier looked straight into the sympathetic eyes of the nun.

"What's your name, Sister?" he asked.

"Sister Margaret Mary."

"Sister Margaret Mary," he echoed. "I'll remember you always."

When she left him at the door, Sister Margaret walked back to the office and placed the sleeping infant in the wait-

The Foundling

ing bassinet. "We'll tend to you, baby," she whispered, untangling the ribbon at the tiny throat.

Her expert fingers explored the child's clothing. She was looking for something. "Sure enough, baby, it's here." She found the note pinned to the baby's shirt. It was unsigned. In the gas light, she read the single line written in pencil. It was simple, short and tragic.

"His mother's name is Mary."

Sister Margaret's lips trembled when she looked at the picture of the Madonna over the bassinet.

"His mother's name is Mary," she whispered. Then the door bell rang again.

It was the young soldier.

"Excuse me, Sister. I forgot something."

"Yes, Mr. Taggart? Won't you come in?"

"I want you to take this for him—for the baby," Paul began, holding out a five dollar bill.

"It's nothing, Sister. Take it," he insisted, as the young nun's face plainly showed her hesitancy.

"Well—thank you, Mr. Taggart." Sister Margaret stood awkwardly twisting the money in her fingers.

"I'd like to see the baby once more, if it's all right with you," Paul said.

"Certainly!" Sister Margaret said. She led him back to the office and her eyes were now twinkling.

Paul stood for a few seconds bending over the sleeping child, tucked in the warmth of its new crib. Straightening, he looked across the corridor into the dimly lighted nursery beyond. "You have a lot of kids in this place."

The Foundling

"Twenty-eight on this floor, including *your* baby, Mr. Taggart."

"Twenty-eight including *my* baby," he repeated the words and for the second time since he returned "home" from war, Paul Taggart smiled.

They crossed the corridor into the dormitory and Sister Margaret led him between the two lines of cribs. "Here's a little China-boy," she whispered.

"Colored babies, too?"

"All colors, all races, Mr. Taggart."

"I guess all kinds of folks get into all kinds of trouble," he said.

"That's right."

Sister Margaret surveyed the young soldier as they returned to the office. He was at least six feet tall. His dark hair, curling at the back of his neck, reminded her of Joey. "I hope you *do* adopt the baby some day, Paul," she said in a burst of intimacy that surprised her.

Paul turned and faced her. A strange, shy look crept into his eyes and his voice betrayed his fears. "Maybe I'll never be able to adopt him, Sister."

"Why not, Mr. Taggart?"

"Because—because the baby will need a mother, and I don't think . . ." Paul's eyes rested upon her face and in that instant the nun knew that the scars of war brand not only a man's body—but his soul.

"Good-by, Sister," he said simply.

"Good-by, Paul. God love you."

Half an hour later, a nun sitting beside a freshly bathed

The Foundling

infant forgot her own grief and loneliness as she played mother to one more tiny, homeless babe. "The Finding of Jesus in the Temple," she whispered, fingering the last decade of the Rosary. Her thoughts mingled with a boy named Paul and a baby whose mother's name was Mary.

Her shadow fell caressingly, protectingly across the cribs all the way to the far wall. "Maybe someday he *will* get married. Maybe someday he will adopt this baby. O please Lord, please help him," she prayed.

Paul? A Sorrowful Mother, a helpless Foundling and a gentle nun united to send a grateful, humble son to seek his own waiting mother.

Chapter 3

PAUL TAGGART sat in the chair facing his mother. It was his second night home, and he noted with secret satisfaction the change in his mother's voice. Tonight she was relaxed and at peace. Her eyes were getting accustomed to see the violences of war stamped upon him. He wanted it this way. He wanted to be accepted without pity or hysteria. Most of all, he wanted her to talk easily, without the fright and pain of last night.

She was even smiling now. "You were always different, Paul."

"What do you mean, Mom?"

"It isn't everyone who can just walk into a church and find a baby-boy, you know."

They laughed. It was their first laugh together since he had come home.

The Foundling

The laugh died away and he said softly, "It gave me a funny feeling."

"I should think it would. Bewildering, wasn't it?"

"Well, not exactly that. I . . . I began to feel he was mine. I wanted him. I wanted to keep him. I guess I still do."

"Son, some day you're going to have children of your own, you know."

Paul felt that familiar twinge of fear and pain and hoped it didn't show.

"I suppose so, Mom," he said. "But I'd like this one, too."

"I imagine if you want him badly enough there are ways of adopting him."

And there it was before them—the subject he most dreaded and about which neither had yet spoken. Ellen. Ellen would have to agree. *If* Ellen would still have him.

It was his mother who broke the silence, simply and directly.

"Ellen wants to see you, Paul," she said.

He felt his mother's eyes studying him. "I'll get around to calling sooner or later."

"She's waiting, Paul. She will be happy again, now you're home."

"Maybe, Mom. Maybe."

"I wouldn't worry about Ellen, son. You know how much she cares."

But he couldn't help worrying about Ellen. He could see her dark brown-flecked eyes and the sweep of her red-gold hair and the swing of her proud head; he could hear the ring of her voice, feel the touch of her hand; and then he

The Foundling

knew the longing to be near her again, the need to share with Ellen those afternoons when they walked for hours, talking, laughing, planning. Sitting here in this room, he hungered for the privileges of being normal again, for winter evenings and a toboggan on a hill, for the snow you lifted in your hands and rubbed against your partner's flushed, cold cheeks, for the ice cream parlor where you caught the reflections of your laughing faces in the cracked mirror, when you both jokingly agreed that you'd make a "peach of a pair."

Again Paul Taggart felt the dread and doubt of the past months press down upon him, leaving him ravaged and drenched in despair. "I can't face her just yet," he muttered. "Not yet."

His mother rose and motioned to his bedroom. "Go inside, Paul. Go ahead."

"What's up?"

"Look for yourself, Paul." Mrs. Taggart smiled.

Paul walked into the room. There he saw a gray tweed suit spread across the bed. He bit his lip—hard. He had to.

His mother stood beside him. "It's the suit you bought before you went away, Paul. I've been saving it just for tonight."

"Looks pretty good."

"Put it on, Paul. And that nice blue tie, the one you never wore."

"Blue was always your favorite color, Mom."

"Ellen's color, too." Mrs. Taggart tried to quiet the tremor in her voice. "Come on, son. You don't want to hurt Ellen. She's waited so long." And to herself, she cried, "So too have

The Foundling

I—so very, very long. Give him back his courage, dear God, make his spirit whole again. Then it won't hurt so much when he looks into the mirror!"

The clock was chiming seven. "All right, Mom. I'll see Ellen." But he said it with effort, without enthusiasm.

An hour later, Paul Taggart turned the last corner that led to Ellen's house. His eyes searched anxiously for the mellow light behind the curtain. It was better to face her at this hour, Paul thought. It was dark. Ordinarily, a fellow wouldn't have to worry about meeting his girl in the sunlight. But Paul kept thinking of his raw scar. That ugly smear across his face looked less raw under gas-light. He had noted that. Several times he had studied himself in mirrors. There were angles you could hold, a posture, a tilt of the head that threw a merciful shadow across the wound and the pain. He had practised it often as he sat in an Army canteen. He had experimented with the small nickel-plated mirror he carried in his pocket. "Yeah, there are certain angles to it," he told himself. "Certain angles you can hold, and people won't look at you twice."

He pushed the house bell and waited. He turned like a shy, hurt animal at bay. He wanted to run away.

Then the door opened.

"Ellen, I'm home," he said.

"Paul!"

Ellen's arms were around him; her hair pressed against his face. He felt her shoulders shake with quiet sobs.

"I'm home," he repeated. "Heck, there's nothing to cry about." And Paul tried to laugh.

The Foundling

Then Ellen lifted her head and looked at Paul. He could feel her eyes running over every inch of him. When she tilted his chin with her fingers, when she forced his head slightly upwards into the direct glare of the hall light, Paul Taggart knew once and for all time that there were no angles clever enough to hide pain from the probing eyes of someone who loved you.

"Got banged up a bit. That's all. But I still got a good left arm."

"Now I know why you didn't write, Paul. You just weren't left-handed! Were you afraid to have someone else write and tell me?"

"Yes."

"Why?"

"Oh, for lots of reasons."

"Did you think . . ." her voice trembled, "were you afraid it would make a difference?"

"It could make a difference, Ellen. You know that."

She was forcing a smile when she lifted her hands to his face. "That's right, Paul. It does make a difference. Tonight, I'm really beginning to love you."

Paul closed his eyes. Sensitively, Ellen's fingers traced the outlines of his face, soothing the jagged scar. Clean, caressing fingers already pulsing with tender mother-mercies to heal the hurt of a man's torn flesh. And while Paul felt those fingers upon his face, his thoughts turned back to the tiny features of the Foundling he had fondled so little time ago. It was good to close one's eyes. It was pleasant and peaceful to be as a little child in need of love and loved.

Chapter 4

Sister Margaret, waiting in her room, barely had time to arrange her habit neatly before she was summoned to the parlor.

As Paul Taggart rose to greet her and the nun saw his broad, boyish grin, she felt Paul's life had already begun to be good again. Today he was dressed as a civilian in a quiet gray cheviot. His eyes sparkled and Sister Margaret immediately felt happy with him. "Gosh, it's good to see you again, Sister."

Sister Margaret took his left hand, secretly pleased at the genuine warmth of his greeting.

Proudly, Paul presented his companion.

"This is Ellen Price, my—my future wife, Sister."

Sister Margaret took Ellen's hand firmly, gently in both her own and felt the strength, surety and sincerity of this tall lovely girl. She knew at once that Paul would never again be lonely, bitter or afraid—not so long as he shared life with Ellen.

"It's good to know you, Ellen," she said, her own blue eyes looking deep into the brown-gold eyes of this girl. And Ellen realized that here was a friend, a friend to help heal not only the frailties of spirit but also the weaknesses and hurts of mind and body. This young nun was perhaps no older than herself. Yet the naturalness, understanding and full nobility of womanhood was like starshine gleaming from out the beautiful eyes of Sister Margaret. "Yes, here is Paul's friend and mine," Ellen said to herself as she felt the Sister's firm fingers cover and hold her own.

The nun, aware of the boy's shyness, asked, "Don't you want to show Ellen your baby, Paul?"

He smiled at her gratefully and nodded. Sister Margaret understood.

They took the elevator to the well babies' nursery. Ellen and Paul stood still, just within the doorway and for a moment neither one said a word. Here was not one baby— but twenty. Here were twenty tiny infants to be cared for each hour of the day. These thoughts raced through Ellen's mind as she stood with Paul seeking *their* baby. Each crib had its baby and its history, each poignant story hidden or only hinted behind the few words written upon the charts.

Sister Margaret stopped beside a bassinet. Its tiny occupant was lying fast asleep, the small fingers curled into tiny fists. Paul bent over the crib and examined the name-band strapped to the baby's wrist. "Peter Lane," he read. "Peter and Paul.

The Foundling

I like that. Sounds fine. Peter Lane. That will be his real name, Sister?"

"That's the name we gave him."

The baby suddenly opened his eyes wide and blue and gazed placidly at the ceiling.

"What do you think of him, Ellen?" Paul never took his eyes from the baby.

"He's a darling, a beautiful baby, Paul."

"And to think that I was the one to find him!" Paul exclaimed proudly. "It's pretty wonderful when you stop to think about it . . ."

"Hey, Peter, look at me. Stop staring at the ceiling. Come on, fella," Paul coaxed as he unwound the diminutive fist and watched the fingers uncurl, then immediately curl again around his straight, strong finger.

The nun lifted Peter and carried him out to the sun porch where Paul, insisting that he could handle the baby as well with one arm as any nurse with two, took the child from her.

"After all, who found him? Who lifted him from his *first* crib? I managed then, didn't I?" Paul challenged. The two women understood and silently thanked God for the will and the way of this boy made man again.

It was a mellow moment. A golden March sun, poised far over New Jersey, flooded the porch with warmth. Deep in the heart of this teeming city, the Foundling Home loomed large and rambling, with its play tools, its walkers, rattles, blocks, and rag dolls strewn about in colorful abandon. It would soon be time to tuck away babies and toys for the

The Foundling

night, but right now, Sister Margaret mused, it was pleasant to be sitting looking at a boy with a baby cradled in his arm and a girl with the sun in her hair, in love with each other, and both in love with the Foundling nestled against the boy's heart.

Ellen broke into the nun's daydream. "Of course, we know we can't adopt the baby now," she began, "but Paul and I know we can afford to care for him in a year or two, Sister."

"That is, if you don't find his parents or relatives," Paul added, in an effort to be perfectly regular about the matter.

"Will you tell us, Sister, just how we should go about adopting Peter?" Ellen asked.

"It's simple, really. When you come to claim Peter, just bring letters from your doctor and from your parish priest; and be prepared to give the names of several people . . ."

Sister Margaret stopped. She had seen once again a streak of fear play upon the scarred face of the soldier.

"Our parish priest . . . but we're not Catholics, didn't I tell you, Sister?"

"Oh," Sister Margaret gasped.

Paul tried to smile, to be composed. He hoped Ellen did not suspect the dread that once again ripped and tore at him.

"You're not mad at us, are you, Sister?"

"Mad? Oh, no, Mr. Taggart . . . Paul." Sister Margaret rattled her beads nervously. "But . . . but that makes it impossible for you to adopt Peter." The words came out in a rush, and they shook her almost as much as she knew they shocked Ellen and Paul.

"Impossible?" Paul and Ellen exclaimed together.

The Foundling

"Yes. You see the baby is a Catholic." She looked pleadingly at Ellen, hoping this loving girl would help her spare Paul more hurt and pain.

But both were puzzled.

Then Sister Margaret attempted to explain. "It's like this, Paul. When a baby is left in a church, that is, a Catholic Church, it becomes officially and automatically a Catholic. You do see, don't you?"

"No, no, I can't, Sister. Suppose he *is* a Catholic. Can't I still adopt him?" Paul asked.

"I'm afraid not," Sister Margaret answered gravely. "Once a child's religion is established, he has a right to be brought up in that religion. Since little Peter is a Catholic, he has a right to be brought up by Catholic foster parents who will teach and guide him in the truths of our religion."

Ellen looked helplessly at Paul.

"But, Sister, we *have* to have him," Paul exclaimed. "Why," his eyes widened in sudden, startling recollection, "why, I *promised* I'd take care of him!"

"You promised, Paul?"

"Yes, Sister, the night I found him. I forgot about it until just now." Then Paul told Ellen and the nun of his promise made to the Sorrowful Mother on that cold December night as he stood before her statue in the Cathedral with his baby tucked under the empty sleeve of his uniform. "I promised Her I'd take care of him," he finished simply.

"And so you did, Paul," Sister Margaret Mary said softly. "You did take care of him. You brought him to the right place."

"But I can do everything you want me to do," Paul insisted. "I'll send him to a Catholic school. I'll bring him to church. I'll . . . I'll . . ."

Sister Margaret looked straight into his eyes and there were tears in her own. She knew Paul meant every word he said. And because she knew it, she was sad. "I believe you, Paul. I know you would. But it's something that can't be helped."

She looked away, then, past the cupolas, past the El, past all the granite horizons of the city. She sighed.

"I believe you, Paul," she repeated. "But it can't be helped." Then, wistfully, she added, "I wish it could!"

Sister Margaret Mary stood at the door, with Peter warm and peaceful in her arms, and waved when Paul and Ellen left. It had all been so wonderful, seemed so right and promised such happiness. And now . . .

"You will come back again, soon, won't you?" she called almost pleadingly after them. But their answer was lost in the hum of the traffic.

Chapter 5

THE FOG hung over the world like a cold, gray shawl that Sunday in November, two and a half years later. Hesitantly, Paul Taggart walked up the steps of St. Rita's. Inside he saw a huge, ceremonious gentleman who hovered over a collection-table strewn with nickels, dimes and quarters. The congregation was standing, and Paul had an uneasy suspicion that he was out of place.

"Is church almost over?" Paul asked the ceremonious gentleman.

The man looked at him in wonderment. "Over! Why, it's just beginning. As a matter of fact, mister, you're five minutes late." The man was bristling like some arch-angelic sergeant-at-arms who had been posted at the outer gates of worship with a railroad watch in one hand and the sword of Sabbatical righteousness in the other. A rumbling wave of sound filled the church as the congregation settled into the pews.

"I don't want to go to Mass," Paul continued above the singing of the *Kyrie.*

"You don't want to . . ."

"No, sir. I'm not a Catholic."

"Oh!" The man gulped and drew back a few paces to study this interesting visitor.

"I'd like to see the pastor, Father Sheerin," Paul continued.

"Father Sheerin is saying Mass right now. You can see him in the sacristy when he's finished." The man indicated the sacristy door with a wave of his arm.

Paul thanked him and moved up the aisle awkwardly. He was about to slip into a vacant seat behind a pillar when the priest chanted a strange phrase. The congregation rose to its feet as one person, and the *Gloria* pealed throbbingly from the organ into the high-vaulted ceiling. Paul decided to retreat to the safety and silence of the sacristy.

William Snoggins Mulrooney, sacristan of St. Rita's Church, was dozing in an old sedilia when Paul entered. Paul did not know that one might go into St. Rita's sacristy at precisely this time every Sunday morning and find Snoggins taking his ritual nap between collections. Snoggins was, *ex officio,* sacristan, porter, acolyte and, by virtue of an explosive formula, exorcist, too. He directed his exorcisms at the altar boys whom he had come to regard as so many necessary evils. They were always making fun of him, especially when they happened upon him in one of his in-between-the-collection moments.

Paul walked lightly toward the sleeping sacristan. Seated

The Foundling

on the old sedilia, Snoggins offered a striking picture of complete collapse. He was endowed by nature with more than a moderate share of flesh and he gave it all the rest possible. His pudgy hands were folded reverently over a wax stained vest, rising and falling in rhythm with a snore that, for the moment, threatened to surpass the best efforts of the choir.

A board creaked under Paul's foot, and Snoggins came slowly to life. First his eyes blinked, then fluttered, then stared vacantly at nothing for a second or two, and finally settled down in focus on the business of sizing up the person who had broken his slumber.

"What do you want, young man?" Snoggins yawned.

"I'd like to wait here for the pastor."

"This is no place to wait for the pastor. This is a sacristy," he yawned again. "People who want to see the pastor usually wait in the rectory."

Paul excused himself and shifted from one foot to the other.

It was when Snoggins saw Paul's empty sleeve that he finally awakened and repented. "Lost your arm in the war?"

"Yes, sir."

"Too bad, son. Too bad." Snoggins lifted himself out of the chair and yawned again. "Sit down," he said gruffly, pointing to the sedilia.

Paul hesitated but felt he should obey.

"I never saw you around here before," the sacristan continued.

"No, sir. I don't belong to your church."

"You mean you're a Protestant?"

"Yes, sir."

Snoggins scratched his head. "Going to take instructions?"

Paul was puzzled. "I don't understand, sir."

"Are you going to become a Catholic?"

"No, sir." Paul's voice was slightly vexed. He resented curiosity.

"Excuse me. I didn't mean to become personal," Snoggins apologized, looking straight at Paul.

"That's all right."

"I'd suggest, however, that if you have anything to discuss with Father Sheerin, you'd better wait in the rectory."

Snoggins was moving to the door when Paul interrupted him. "I wanted to see the pastor about getting a baby."

"A baby!" Snoggins bellowed without turning.

"Well, a little boy. He's almost three years old."

Snoggins walked back to Paul with heightened interest. "You mean you want to adopt a baby?"

"Yes, sir."

"Well, why don't you go to an orphanage?" Snoggins asked.

Paul went into lengthy detail about the situation at the orphanage. "You see, I'm married, sir. Two and a half years, now. And my wife and I . . ." Paul stopped, embarrassed.

"I understand. You mean you can't have children."

"That's right. And besides, this little boy likes us. We've been visiting him regularly for the past two years."

Snoggins thrust his pudgy hands into his vest and weighed the problem. "And why did you come to see Father Sheerin?"

"I thought a priest could persuade the Sisters to let us adopt this boy. My wife and I will guarantee the priest of this parish that we'll do everything expected of us. We'll bring Peter here every Sunday to church. We'll send him to St. Rita's school. We'll do everything, sir, if they'll only allow us to adopt him."

"You got a job?" Snoggins asked. "You financially responsible?"

"Oh, yes," Paul replied hastily. "I have a job with an insurance company. A good solid job. Not selling. It's a desk job." He was eager to reassure this curious, friendly man.

Snoggins stared intently at Paul. There was a pathetic yearning in the young man's voice that touched a soft chord in the ponderous sacristan.

"Look, mister," Snoggins began. "I can tell you right now that there's nothing Father Sheerin can do for you. Catholic children can never be adopted by non-Catholic parents and Protestant children must be entrusted to Protestant parents or guardians. You're wasting your time if you think you can make them bend their rules down there at the orphanage. Why," Snoggins clapped his pudgy hands together for emphasis, "not even the Archbishop himself can pull strings for you on a deal like that."

A large Thomas clock ticked monotonously and, for the first time, Paul was aware of the stale odor of incense and of the faded portraits of severe ecclesiastics staring coldly at him from the drab wall. He felt like lifting himself out of the chair and running madly out of the sacristy, out of the

The Foundling

church, far from all this correct and rigid bondage of Roman rules and precepts and practices. He took a deep breath and stared belligerently at the bulky sacristan.

"Excuse me, sir. I think I'll go now," his voice was cold as he rose out of the sedilia.

Snoggins pushed him back roughly into the broad chair. "Wait a minute, mister. I want to get this straight."

Paul glowered at Snoggins.

"You say you like this little boy?"

"Yes, sir."

"You'd like to have him around you all the time—all the rest of your life?"

"Yes, sir."

"All right. Listen to me." Snoggins thrust his fat hands into his vest pockets and cocked his head at an angle that was portentous of big news. "Do you have any friends who are Catholics?" The question was wrapped in sly and mysterious innuendo.

"Friends who are Catholics?" Paul echoed impatiently. "Sure, I have friends who are Catholics. Plenty of them."

Snoggins cocked a masterful eyebrow and his next question came with deliberate suspense. "Do you have any friends, that is, *Catholic* friends, who might be interested in adopting a boy about three years old?"

The words seeped in slowly and Paul's eyes brightened as they caught the implication.

"You mean . . . ?

"I mean it's a very simple matter for two Catholics to adopt this Peter you're talking about. And after *they* adopt

· 41 ·

him . . ." Snoggins snapped his fat fingers and left the conclusion dangling dramatically in the air.

Paul smiled slowly at the delicious roguery of this pseudo-Solomon.

"I see what you mean, sir. All I have to do is get a Catholic couple to adopt Peter, and *then* . . ."

Snoggins snapped his fingers again. "And then there's nothing to stop you and your wife from borrowing the boy for, let's say, two or three or twenty years." He looked guiltily behind him as if expecting an avenging angel to descend upon him. But in the next moment he forgot his fears and, thrusting a wad of snuff into each nostril, he waited under the glow of his own merry benediction for Paul's final *imprimatur*. "What do you think of the idea?"

"I think it's a swell idea!" Paul exclaimed, rising, while the beaming sacristan clasped Paul's one hand in both of his.

William Snoggins Mulrooney flicked a scale of liturgical wax from his vest. "It's nothing at all. Nothing at all. You know, we Protestants and Catholics have to stick together."

Paul laughed.

"As a matter of fact, Protestants, Catholics, and Jews ought to stick together," Snoggins added with the authoritative air of an Atlas upon whose fleshy shoulders rested the turbulent weight of the destiny of the League of Nations.

"I agree with you heartily," Paul said. "You'll never know how much you have helped me, sir. By the way, what's your name?"

"William Mulrooney. But you can call me Snoggins."

"And mine is Paul Taggart."

The Foundling

They shook hands again.

When Paul left the sacristy by the side door, Snoggins took his beads out of his pocket and looked sheepishly at Murillo's Madonna hanging, as usual, above the aluminum fixtures of the sacrarium.

"Now you understand, Mary, that I don't mean a bit of harm," he began in a whisper that was half way between prayer and soliloquy. "After all, there's no rule that can't stand a little bendin', between you and me, and God knows that young man is as fine a fellow as you ever laid eyes on, even though he *is* a Protestant."

Snoggins looked like an apprehensive bad boy in the presence of a Queen.

"But to make sure, Mary, I'd better say an act of contrition . . . just in case," he added, blessing himself.

The fog, which had been lying heavily over the world, brightened momentarily under the persistent sun.

"It's time to take up the collection," Snoggins breathed, and he walked through the sacristy door with the plodding grace of God's heaven-hound into the hushed assemblage of St. Rita's.

Chapter 6

SEVEN WEEKS later, on a bright cold morning in January, there was skirmish in the air. The sun had risen and struck the eastern battlements of the city, leaving a million glass windows flashing like brassy shields. The vast metropolitan world of concrete and steel, flailed by rain that had frozen in the night, was now standing rigid and greaved in the shining armor of ice.

Sitting in a deep leather chair before Vincent Hughes, Paul Taggart waved his arm excitedly. "There isn't a thing to worry about, Vince. All we have to do is get Peter at ten o'clock. The papers have been signed. You and Maureen have been approved. Everything's set."

Vincent Hughes, tall, middle-aged, and conservative, paced the floor of his apartment. "I'll admit, Paul, it sounded like a good idea at first. You know there's nothing I wouldn't do for you and Ellen. But to be frank, I don't feel too good about this. Adopting a child under false pretenses is . . . well," Hughes paused to inspect his cigar, "it's not strictly honest, Paul."

Paul bit his lip reflectively. "Do we have to go into all that again, Vince? I promised you nothing's going to happen to the boy."

"I know, Paul. I understand perfectly."

"When the people from the Foundling Home visit, we'll bring Peter over here and no one will ever know the difference."

Hughes, thinking about the preparations Paul had made for Peter's arrival, smiled indulgently at the enthusiasm of his young friend. During the past week, Paul had bought dozens of religious books in a store on Barclay Street. He had even bought a large bronze crucifix because, as he had put it, "I saw one hanging in the room where Peter slept."

"Besides," Paul continued urgently, "if it comes to a showdown, I'm only borrowing Peter from you. Even Mr. Mulrooney at Saint Rita's knows there's no harm in that."

Hughes flicked his cigar ash into a pewter tray and muttered an unintelligible malediction on the candle-snuffing sacristan.

"I still have a feeling, Paul, that I'm getting myself involved in something. My wife is beginning to feel the same way, too."

Maureen Hughes rose from the sofa and nervously emptied ashtrays. Paul noted her troubled look. There was a dismal silence broken only by the muffled babbling of coffee from the kitchen.

The Foundling

Finally, Paul lifted himself out of the chair and faced Hughes. His scarred face was grim and purposeful. "Vince, I'd like to ask you one question."

"What is it, Paul?"

"Would you and Maureen be afraid to trust your own child to me?"

Hughes smiled easily. "Not in the least, Paul."

"If you wouldn't be afraid to trust your own child to me, why are you worrying now about Peter?"

Hughes bit deeply into his cigar and seemed to be deliberating. He looked slowly from his wife to Taggart and, finally, said with a shrug, "Oh, well, so long as we've gone this far, we might as well go through with it."

Mrs. Hughes was frowning in the doorway. "Coffee's ready," she announced, and walked hurriedly out of the room.

Twenty minutes later, when they were ready to leave, she remarked, "If you don't mind, Vincent, I think I'll stay here."

"But we'll be back in less than an hour, Maureen. You'll enjoy the ride and, besides, they're expecting both of us."

Maureen folded her napkin deliberately. "Really, Vincent, I'd rather not." Hughes stared thoughtfully at her.

As they were getting into their coats, Paul repeated the nicer details of strategy. "All you have to do, Vince, is get Peter into the car. If they see me, they'll suspect something, so I'll wait around the corner, south side."

Mrs. Hughes sighed unhappily when they walked to the door.

"Come on, Maureen, cheer up," Paul beamed. "This is

The Foundling

going to be the happiest day of your life! And of Ellen's. And look! It'll do me a lot of good. Insurance companies like their employees to have children. I might even get a raise. If I do," he added seriously, "I'll put every penny of it in a savings bank for Peter."

But Maureen did not join them. When they walked out the door, she sank wearily into her chair. Left alone in the bright silence of the room, she began to sense again vague but persistent misgivings.

It was very confusing and irritating. Peter and Paul and Catholicism and Protestantism were feverishly mixed, somehow, in this quiet moment in the room. Not that she had thought of it that way at first. No indeed! Then it was all quite adventuresome and challenging. It was a pleasantly harmless bit of intrigue that one subscribed to after dinner over coffee and a pre-prohibition *creme de menthe*. It was an exuberant pledge, signed and sealed in a moment of gay good-fellowship. After all, Paul did need the child. Anyone could sense that. And Paul was such a good friend.

But Maureen Hughes, listening to their footsteps descending the stairs, was troubled that morning. The compelling voice of that small thing called conscience insisted on intruding upon her complacency. Perhaps, she and Vincent had been a trifle precipitate about the matter. Perhaps they were making a serious mistake.

Still, there *was* such a thing as loyalty to a friend.

She walked nervously to the window.

Her dark eyes, brooding with indecision, were attracted, momentarily, by thin strips of ice slipping from the trees

The Foundling

and breaking on the street below. The world was melting slowly under the glare of the mounting January sun. A few feet from her window, a sharp oak twig, tipped thickly with ice, was shaking and glinting like a stiff rapier in the high breeze. Suddenly, she found herself wondering how long it would take the sun to free it from the ice.

She found it impossible to pursue this innocent distraction. Something painfully provocative was beating against her brain. Her darting eyes swept the modest apartment. This domestic kingdom, set to the polished whorls of walnut and oak; this chaste, dusted realm of Royal Daulton and other exotic bric-a-brac; this chamber of bourgeois compromise, running from the stiff elegance of Louis Quinze to pink celluloid bulldogs from a Woolworth counter; all this rented, inhabited space called home became instantly cold and dead.

Suddenly, she was trembling.

"My God, I don't even have a crucifix in the house," she whispered. And she was thinking of Paul—Paul, a Protestant, who paid twelve dollars for a crucifix to hang before the eyes of little Peter. Her fingers twitched nervously in the beads at her throat. She was thinking of herself and Vincent. They were Catholics, of course. By birth and education, they were Catholics. They contributed regularly to the support of their pastor; they went to missions; they even made an occasional novena. They *did* miss Sunday Mass once in a while when the weather was *very* stormy but . . .

The picture of a scarred boy carrying home religious books from Barclay Street for an orphan shattered her complacency.

The Foundling

Her conscience, long blanketed in a cold, parochial masquerade was stripped at last.

Outside the world was getting brighter. The twig, dripping under the high sun, was still encased in its sheath of ice. Drop by drop the cold, translucent beads of water fell to the ground. And then, suddenly, this single rapier, thrusting at the broad might of the insistent sun, was stripped clean and free. The ice fell and splintered into a thousand diamonds at the base of the broad oak.

The duel was done.

Maureen Hughes saw her husband cranking the car. In an instant, she dashed to the door, and ran quickly down the stairs.

"Vincent!" she called.

"What's the trouble, Maureen?"

"I'd like to see you for a minute."

Paul Taggart waved to her from his seat in the automobile. "Did you change your mind, Maureen?" he shouted. "We've got plenty of room in the car."

"No, Paul, I'm not going."

Vincent Hughes walked back to the house. "What's on your mind, Maureen?"

"Come in here. In the hall."

"You're acting strangely this morning."

"I can't help it, Vince. You've got to listen to me. We can't go through with this—this hoax."

"Will you stop worrying about a lot of foolish details?"

"They're not details and you know it, Vincent. This is a matter of conscience."

The Foundling

"We've already discussed that."

"I want you to tell Paul that we can't take that child from the Foundling Home."

Hughes showed irritation. "I'm not telling Paul anything. We've gone this far, and I'm not backing out now."

"I refuse to give my consent, Vince."

"Sure, you refuse to give your consent," Hughes cut in ironically. "The papers are signed. We've been investigated and approved, and now you refuse to give your consent. Well," Hughes was breathing heavily, "it's too late to back out."

"It's never too late to be honest, Vince."

"Forget it and stop worrying."

"Then you refuse to listen to me?"

"Go upstairs and take it easy, Maureen, you're going to catch cold."

"Please, Vincent. Listen to me. We can't . . ."

But Hughes was already walking back to the automobile. Maureen watched the car as it chugged down the avenue and out of sight. Slowly she retraced her steps up the stairs. She walked mechanically into the apartment, past the chairs, through the kitchen, into the parlor. There was no deviation, no hesitation in her movements. She went to the telephone.

"I'm sorry, Vincent," she whispered. And while she was lifting the receiver, she added quietly and definitely: "I'm sorry, Paul."

Chapter 7

IT SHOULD have been an ordinary day in January. It should have followed the usual routine of the Foundling: visitors, feedings, charts, check-ups, reports, and the daily official business. But for Sister Margaret Mary this day was different. Three-year-old Peter Lane was scheduled to leave the orphanage that morning!

Automatically, she packed Peter's clothing neatly in a box.

"You'll miss Peter, won't you, Sister?" a nurse asked.

"Yes. Yes, I shall, Miss Johnson," Sister Margaret answered, trying to sound casual for, no one, not even Nurse Johnson, was ever to suspect. After all, this was customary procedure. Every week of the year, homeless babies were brought to the Hospital to be nursed, tended, boarded out; every week of the year new infants were left to take their places in perpetual streams of abandoned and saved human beings.

The Foundling

On the books, cold, clear statistics stated the story. There was only so much room. There were only so many beds. If babies were not adopted, foster homes must be found for them. "Would you be kind enough, with the kindness of Christ, to board a baby in your home." Thus read the leaflets distributed by the Foundling Hospital. "We ask you to offer a temporary home to an abandoned baby. You will receive a regular allotment from the institution." Thus spoke the social workers. It was, necessarily, a factual procedure. "Your check will come on or after the twenty-eighth day of the month, madam. Receipted bills for doctors' visits, medicines and so forth will be gladly paid by the Foundling Home, madam."

This was the routine recital, the keen knife of necessity and efficiency cutting the intangible threads that moored a baby to its borrowed crib in the orphanage.

No, Miss Johnson was not to suspect. Sister Margaret was remembering the Superior's injunction. The Sisters were not to cultivate any special or particular affection for the children in their care. It was unwise, unkind and unfair.

"All children are to be treated alike," Sister Superior had said in a community conference. The nuns, sitting rigidly in the chairs, listened, showing no spark nor stir of emotion. "You will find, Sisters, that human nature tends easily to things that please and gratify the affections. But you must know and understand that the work to which you are devoting your lives demands not only the strongest sense of attachment, but also the most courageous sense of detachment." Sister Superior, twirling the black watch cord around her finger, stood at the conference desk, wonderfully wise and impressive. "Upon the face of every child, diseased or well, white or black, you are expected to find the features of Christ."

These were not mere mouthings from the wise lips of Sister Superior. To this ideal of Charity, Sister Superior was trained; to this sublime expression of Charity she trained her nuns.

And so, Sister Margaret, leaning over Peter's crib that day, was deeply troubled. "Dear God," she breathed, "I do tend all the children with affection. But Peter—forgive me—I love him! O merciful Mother, do you, you must understand!"

Miss Johnson stirred behind her.

"You will please take Peter to the office now, Miss Johnson. He can wait for his foster parents there. And I . . ." Sister Margaret hesitated. At that moment, the past three years crushed down upon her. She was dreaming again in the cold, early hours of a December morning, dreaming of her brother Joey, so young, so confident, so carefree, and suddenly—so dead somewhere in France. And then the memory of the other soldier, standing shyly before her, a wee babe lying against his fast-beating heart.

"You've meant happiness to me, Peter," she whispered wistfully. "You will never know, but you helped me to be resolute in my religious vocation." And because Miss Johnson was still standing close upon her heels, and because she was remembering the injunctions of Sister Superior, aloud she said simply, "Good-by, Peter. God bless you!" Then Sister Margaret walked quickly out of the nursery, her hood

The Foundling

shading the tears in her eyes, the folds of her habit hiding her trembling hands as she fingered her rosary.

Fifteen minutes later, while she was piling cakes of soap in a cupboard in the Isolation Unit, Sister Superior discovered her. "Sit down, Sister Margaret, sit down. One more morning like this and I'll collapse," the Superior began, sinking into a chair beside Sister Margaret. "We just received a phone call from Mrs. Hughes." The young nun sat still scarcely breathing, as she listened to the Superior reconstruct the conversation, word for word. The disclosure of the ruse had shaken the aging nun. "In all my years at the Foundling Home, Sister Margaret, never have I experienced anything like this and God knows I've had some experiences." She rose and walked slowly to the window. A soft ivory haze filtering through the lace curtains fell upon her pale face now quivering, worn, and sad.

"Mr. Hughes will be here any minute," she said. "This is going to be very unpleasant. There is, of course, only one thing we can do." The Superior looked quickly at the young nun. "I want you to handle this, Sister Margaret. You're young and capable, yet kind." She turned again to the window and added wearily, "Right now, I'd like to make a bid for a permanent assignment in a leper colony."

Ten minutes later Sister Margaret was summoned to the parlor. She sped down the corridor shaken by the shock of her knowledge and the ordeal she must face. And the nun knew she was almost as guilty as Paul—guilty of wanting to care for Peter herself. Her thoughts raced with her. "Poor Paul, he must love and need Peter so very, very much!"

The Foundling

Vincent Hughes rose to greet her, smiling and composed.

"Good morning, Mr. Hughes." Sister Margaret hoped the trembling of her heart was not echoed in her voice.

"It's good to see you again, Sister Margaret. I'm sorry Mrs. Hughes couldn't come, but if Peter is ready . . ."

"Mr. Hughes, this morning we received a phone call." It was a simple sentence. But it left the nun breathless.

Vincent Hughes smiled and waited.

"That phone call told me of a strange set of circumstances surrounding your status as adoptive parents." That was the particular line she had practised a few minutes ago in her room.

Even before Sister Margaret went any further Vincent Hughes guessed the answer—Maureen! But he listened until the nun had finished.

"Is that the truth, Mr. Hughes?" Sister Margaret asked, trying to be gentle and firm.

"Yes, it's the truth, Sister. We wanted to do it for Paul. We didn't realize how wrong it could be. We really didn't. Paul wanted and needed Peter. We wanted to help him and Ellen. I'm sorry. Believe me."

The man lowered his eyes under the steady gaze of the nun. Sister Margaret rose. "Under the circumstances, Mr. Hughes, we cannot let you have Peter for adoption. I am sure you understand. And when you leave, will you please tell Mr. Taggart I'd like to see him—and soon?"

"I'll tell him, Sister. And I hope you'll forgive—all of us. If we did wrong, Sister, it was from ignorance and a deep desire to help devoted friends and a baby they love. Please,

Sister, be charitable to Paul. He needs your help—more, much more, than he needs a lecture."

Ten minutes later, Sister Margaret studied the set, stern face of Paul Taggart.

"You wanted to see me," Paul's voice was strained, cold.

"You almost succeeded, Paul, didn't you?" Sister Margaret said gently.

"I suppose you're glad," he said, bitterly.

"No, I'm not glad. I'm unhappy, Paul. Very. For you, for Peter, for myself!"

But Paul was looking far beyond the young nun, far into the past. He did not see the tears well up and spill from her eyes, now deep violet in their misty sympathy; and because he saw before his brooding eyes the death-masks of his comrades, he feared these would again rouse to beset him if he could not have Peter. Paul Taggart's heart was again lonely and afraid and he was angry and biting.

"I suppose you thought I'd come to you and apologize for trying to get my baby back," he said. "But I won't because I'm not sorry. I'm fed up with all this nonsense, this sham and pretense, or whatever it should be called!"

Sister Margaret's fingers tightened on her beads. "*What* nonsense? *What* sham, Paul?"

Paul stared at Sister Margaret belligerently. "*You* are the one to answer that. *You* are the one who preaches charity and love and tolerance!" He flung his words into the nun's face. If the words had been knives, they would have cut and wounded less.

A moment seeming like eternity enveloped them in hostile

silence. Then the nun regained her composure and spoke, this time softly, pleadingly. "Let us be honest with one another, Paul. Let us admit we are faced with a problem bigger than you, or Vincent Hughes, or Peter, or me."

"And what problem *is* bigger than that?" he challenged.

"Religion, Paul."

It was, she thought, a cold, formal word, provocative, formidable, frightening,—a word that misunderstood, misused and mispracticed had divided whole peoples, empires, continents, and threatened disruption to a world that it was supposed to save!

Paul's face had lost none of its misery, but as he stood straight and tall and defiant, looking down upon this child-like nun who for three years had been mother to *his* precious Peter, his face became less violent, his voice less insolent. For Paul was remembering again. But this time he saw a curly-headed, blond baby-boy, tousled and tired from play. Peter, sleepy and happy, Peter learning to talk, to walk, run and play. Peter Lane who now would never be Peter Taggart.

Sister Margaret, looking up into his scarred, hurt face, longed to heal this man, still boy—longed to heal the wounds of his mind that were deeper than the scar on his face. But wisely she knew that such hurts as his took longer to wash away than the brief span of time left them today. So she said quietly, "I'm sorry, Paul. I am helpless to do anything for you. You can't have Peter because—because you are not a Catholic." It was the wrong thing to say, she knew; she had meant to be short and kind, but she sounded only curt and, yes, she thought, "intolerant."

The Foundling

"Is that all you have to say—smug in the security of your righteousness!" Paul was angry again. The scar on his pathetic face became a livid, searing flame across his cheek. It looked, Sister Margaret thought, as if the gash were still shedding its rich red drops of blood in the agony of unbelief, torment and grief.

Sympathy and sadness overwhelmed her. There was so much she yearned to say, so little time to say it. So she said only, "Yes, Paul, that's all."

But this time, in a voice as raw as his wound, Paul answered:

"You don't love a kid—or, or anyone, just because he's a Catholic, or a Protestant or a Mohammedan, do you? I don't love Ellen because we belong to the same church or share the same house. I love Peter because—because he's mine!" Sturdy, strong, straight-legged Peter, his blond curly hair tumbling across his laughing blue eyes; his firm fingers tugging at Paul's; his left hand coaxing him to play a game or tell him a story; Peter drowsy-eyed, tired, yet begging him to stay with him just a little longer—*these* were the things that made Peter his, made it *right* for them to be together always.

Sister Margaret understood his mood and guessed his memories. She wanted to help. She dreaded hurting him again. So carefully, quietly, this time she chose her words, "No, Paul, you're right, you don't love a baby or anyone just because he's a Catholic, or because he's of your own religion or any religion. And sometimes—very often—you may love someone even more deeply if you do not share his faith. You call me uncharitable, intolerant, a sham. You think because I am vested in the cloak of a nun, I do not possess the understanding or the instincts of a normal human being. You think because I do not tell you all religions are the same, or that each is like the other, that I am intolerant. But were I to say these things and you would call me tolerant, I would then, Paul, truly be a sham—a hypocrite."

The nun's steady gaze captured and held rapt Paul's burning eyes. "Do you not confuse tolerance with compromise?" she asked. "Are you not now running unwittingly with those who would destroy us and our way of life as falsely they compromise truth in the name of tolerance? This new and modern gospel of tolerance, Paul, is not a virtue. It is the vice of indifferentism! Did God say 'Thou shalt tolerate the Lord thy God'? Did He say 'Thou shalt tolerate thy neighbor'? Think Paul—think. The word *He* used was 'love'."

Thus they stood, two who yearned to be one as friends, cleaved by the axe, religion. And the destiny of the towheaded boy was for them a symbol of all humanity, shunted and sacrificed because peoples of different beliefs refused to respect the good faith and the good works of others. And neither the aching heart of the young nun, nor the broken heart of the young veteran could know that in less than two decades, godless leaders, compromising truth and justice in their mad march to power, would attack all religions and religion itself, and contemptuous of human life and happiness drench the whole world in the obscene waste of war.

Chapter 8

PAUL HAD been standing, coldly erect, staring into space. Slowly he sank into a chair opposite Sister Margaret. There was something of resignation in the gesture, something, Sister Margaret felt, that indicated a softening in Paul's attitude if not a complete acceptance of the situation he faced. The hostility that had surrounded him like cold invisible armor was dissipating; in its stead the hurt and the sorrow and the searching prevailed.

"Do you want to see him, Paul?" she asked.

"No. No, Sister, not now. I don't think I could."

"Paul," she continued, "you've been coming here a good deal these past years and yet you don't really know much about us, do you? You've seen Peter and you talk to me, but you've never paid much attention to the others who work and live here, have you? I think if you knew more about the

Foundling you'd understand more about Peter—and yourself and Ellen."

"Perhaps you're right, Sister."

"Have you a few minutes, Paul?" she asked.

"I feel as if I had forever." His reply was slow and lost.

"It won't take that long," she smiled.

And then she told him something of the Foundling Hospital to which she was dedicating her life and which had taken Peter to its bosom that cold December night which now seemed long ago.

She told him of Sister Irene, Foundress of the Foundling, and it was a shock to her that Paul who had been here so often had never heard of her. For the story of Sister Irene, so familiar to the young novice now relating it, had in it the stuff of legend or even miracle. Born Catherine FitzGibbon, of well-to-do Irish parents, she came to New York only to succumb in 1849 to one of the plagues that in those days so often ravaged the city. This time it was Asiatic cholera and Catherine FitzGibbon was given up for dead by her family and physicians. But Catherine was not dead; she could hear and understand every word spoken in her presence but by no amount of will could she utter a sound, or move a muscle. She lay on her bed and heard her family discuss with the undertaker the manner of her interment for in those days of terror, burial was immediate.

"She prayed, Paul," Sister Margaret said. "She prayed and vowed to consecrate herself to God if she were saved. They put her in the casket, Paul, and the undertaker was just about to close it when he noticed her eyelids flickering.

The Foundling

She lived, Paul, and she carried out her vows and this building—she made an all-comprising gesture—"is the result of her lifework."

She told Paul that at the age of twenty-seven Catherine petitioned to be admitted to the order of the Sisters of Charity. It was after the Civil War and there was poverty and disease and crime in New York. Most appalling to Sister Irene, her name in religion, was the frightening rise of infanticide and abandonment of babies. Every morning on porches, on the steps of churches, even in ash cans babies were found exhausted and dying. The city had no means of taking care of them; they were generally taken to the Almshouse where many died. Sister Irene begged her Superior, Mother Jerome, to permit her to found an asylum but Mother Jerome had no funds. Finally Mother Jerome gave her consent and with it a five-dollar bill, which was "all she could afford." That was the beginning of the Foundling Hospital.

"When we tell that story," said Sister Margaret, "we usually refer to Saint Teresa of whom you probably have not heard either. Centuries ago Saint Teresa was faced with the same problem and announced she would start an orphanage with six ducats. She was laughed at but she replied, 'I know six ducats and Teresa are nothing; but six ducats, Teresa, and God are everything!'

"It was like that with the Foundling. Sister Irene slaved, she received contributions from Protestants and Catholics alike; she and her Sisters worked in incredibly inadequate quarters down on Twelfth Street; finally she got the New York Legislature to promise one hundred thousand dollars if the same sum could be raised by private contributions. God and the people of New York blessed her and this"—she gestured again—"was built. You are sitting in a building dedicated to humanity that started with a five-dollar bill and God's blessing, Paul."

Paul was listening, half-attention, because, while the story was not without interest and the repose and the calm voice of Sister Margaret soothed him, all this seemed remote from his problem, from Ellen's and from Peter's. What would happen to Peter now?

Sister Margaret was quick to sense his thoughts.

"Excuse me, Paul," she said. "I love history and I get wound up in it, especially in the history of this place. I'll tell you more about it some other time, or I can give you some booklets we have here and you can read them and the scrap albums of newspaper clippings and letters when you have time. I want to tell you now a little about how we operate today and what we try to do for the children here . . . children like your Peter.

"They come to us in every way imaginable. Sometimes," she smiled quietly, "a soldier rings our bell and gives us one. We used to have a cradle outside the door, but we don't do that any more. We take care of the mother, too, when we can. Sometimes we can find a job for her, or set her up doing sewing or part-time housework, anything that will bring in a little money and still allow her time to look after her child. If she's sick we try to nurse her to health. This hospital is for the mother just as much as for the child. We do everything possible to find the mother and bring her and her child together. We want the mother to *be* a mother because that means happiness for both of them. Sometimes we are even able to persuade the father to return. When we have established a real family unit, when we have been lucky enough to do that, Paul, almost always it has worked out happily. Of course, we don't always know the parents. There are the cases of abandonment—like Peter—where we take the child right in.

"And I think you can tell from looking at Peter that we bring them up all right." She was smiling then, but suddenly she turned serious again. "The trouble, Paul, is we are always crowded. So we try to find proper foster parents for children like Peter, and if after a year nobody has claimed him, he may legally be adopted. I don't have to tell you that we investigate the adopting parents pretty thoroughly. Mr. Hughes must have told you."

A short time ago she would not have dared refer to the Hughes and the attempted subterfuge. Now she noted with pleasure that Paul accepted the allusion casually and with no evident emotion. The storm seemed to have passed, but there was still a point to make.

"You know that this is a Catholic institution, Paul," she said, "but did you know that every other baby brought here is a Protestant? One Protestant, one Catholic, one Protestant, one Catholic—that's how it works. Unless of course the mother leaves definite religious instructions."

"And I have the luck to draw a Catholic," muttered Paul. It was the first time he had spoken and Sister Margaret winced to hear him brooding again.

The Foundling

"You forget, Paul. I told you before. You found Peter in a Catholic church. That makes him a Catholic automatically."

"Well, what about the Jews?" Paul asked still with a touch of surliness. "Why do none of the kids become Jews?"

"The Jewish community in this city long ago gave up its right to have what I suppose you could call a tri-partite agreement," she answered. "They felt they had adequate facilities of their own, and they preferred it that way. If a child comes to us and we have indication that his mother wants him brought up in the Jewish religion we take care of him until we can give him to the care of the proper Jewish authorities."

"That's fair enough, I guess," Paul said. "But about Peter, what's going to happen to Peter?"

"Peter's growing up. If no one adopts him, very soon he'll be going to Mount Mary, down on Staten Island. There he'll get an education, learn a trade, have a chance to earn some money. He may become a mechanic, a farmer, a draughtsman, oh, anything. It's beautiful out there, Paul. Most New Yorkers don't know Staten Island. Only a short—and exciting—ferry ride from Manhattan, and then real country. I do hope Peter goes there, Paul, and I do hope you will visit him. You will both love it, I know."

The conversation stopped there with each looking far away to a Peter growing up to adolescence and manhood, learning the trade or profession best fitted to him, taking his place as a citizen of his country and of his world.

Paul rose. "Thank you, Sister," he said. "You've done me a lot of good; you've explained a lot. I understand now."

The Foundling

Sister Margaret accompanied him to the door.

"I'll pray for our Peter," she said as he paused on the threshold. "We'll expect great things from him."

"President of the United States?" Paul was grinning.

"Why not?" she asked in utmost seriousness. "Two of our youngsters became Governors of their states."

PART 2

Chapter 9

PETER LANE and Paul Taggart stood together one Sunday evening in early September on the knoll overlooking the fields of Mount Mary. The trees would soon be turning to the sad and scarlet splendor of autumn and the farm tools of June, July, and August stacked in the shed. The unpleasant prospect of pencils and books was looming on the calendar.

"These are my fields," Peter told Mr. Taggart. "I worked these fields with Jim Randall and the farm boys. Down there to the left of the water tower, see it, that was the potato patch."

Mr. Taggart looked, but thirteen-year-old Peter, full of the fervor of a farmer, suspected that he did not quite appreciate the glory of a potato patch. So they sat on the grass as he described the wondrous process. It had begun on a morning full of sunshine when he sat with Jim Randall outside the root cellar, burlap over their knees and seed potatoes spread on the ground.

"All you have to do, Mr. Taggart, is cut a potato so that you get at least two eyes in each slice. That's what Jim Randall said."

"Did you plant those potatoes, Peter?"

"Yes, Mr. Taggart. We planted them. Jim Randall and myself."

Paul, remembering the Peter of two summers ago who wanted to grow up to be a fireman and drive a hook-and-ladder truck, smiled at the boy's new enthusiasm. "You really like farming, don't you?"

"I sure do, Mr. Taggart."

Then he described to him the cultivating of potatoes that began gently at first, when the young stalks were barely lifted out of the ground. He told about the deeper cultivations that followed with the dirt running out in skirls from the V teeth. The shovel plowing came later when the plants, thick and strong, could stand the spray of the loam flying up, right and left, to make the mound. Finally, he told Paul about the strange withering of all that was once green and fresh, when the white blossoms were dying on the plants, and the summer was slipping into earlier twilights.

"These stalks get blackish, Mr. Taggart. Blackish and brownish. A week ago, you would think that everything was dead out there on the potato patch. It was the worst field you could look at. No furrows. Nothing. Just dried up stalks lying everywhere. But you know what?"

The Foundling

"What, Peter?"

"Just when you think everything is dead, that's when the potatoes are fully grown. Isn't nature wonderful?"

"It sure is wonderful, Peter."

And it *was* wonderful. The stalks were pulled; the earth was dug and searched; brown multitudes of potatoes were left lying in mounds for the boys with the burlap sacks. Then the full carts were drawn back to the root cellar and unloaded. At the end of the day, with a pleasant sigh of weariness and gratification Randall packed his pipe and said, "Boys, we've got enough spuds to last us till the robins come back in the spring."

All this was satisfying—and sad, too, now that the trees were telling the approach of winter—and of school. Peter sighed. He wanted to be up and across the fields in an unending succession of summer mornings, driving a horse with a harrow or a rake rattling behind him.

"Summer's over, Mr. Taggart," he said at last.

Mr. Taggart lay back on the grass looking up at the sky. A distant swirl of crows went jeering and tumbling into the sunset. Peter's eyes followed them wistfully. He almost wished that he could be one of them. To be a crow was to be beyond the reach of regulations and bells, he thought. It would be nice winging off into the evening with no thought of books or pencils.

"You really want to be a farmer, Peter?" Mr. Taggart's voice broke in on his thoughts.

"Yes."

"More than anything else in the world?"

The Foundling

"Yes, I want to be a farmer more than anything else. I want to be like Jim Randall. Someday I'll have my own house. And I'll have a room for you and Mrs. Taggart. I'll have silos, painted silver like the Mansfield farm. I'll have my barns painted silver, too, Mr. Taggart. And do you know how many cows I'll have?"

"How many?"

"Two hundred, maybe. Maybe three hundred."

"That's going to be a big herd, Peter."

"I'm going to have the biggest herd in the world. All Holsteins."

Mr. Taggart sat up then and looked at Peter for a long time before he spoke. "You're getting old now. You'll soon be leaving Mount Mary."

"I'm going to wait until I am sixteen."

"Then what are you going to do, Peter?"

"I'll get a job in New York. When I make enough money, I'll buy a farm somewhere."

Paul Taggart lit a cigarette and blew the smoke over Peter's head before he asked the question. "Peter, did anyone ever want to adopt you?"

"Me?" Peter laughed. "Oh, no. Most people want to adopt girls, you know," he added seriously.

"They do?"

"Yes. People like to fuss and girls are nicer to dress up with ribbons and things," Peter explained. Then he added, "That's what Sister Margaret thinks, anyway. But she says *she'd* pick a boy if she were going to adopt anyone."

The Foundling

Paul smoked in silence.

"I'm glad no one ever wanted to adopt me," the boy continued.

"Why, Peter?"

Peter's eyes followed the flight of a butterfly as he answered. "I always wanted to be adopted by you, Mr. Taggart."

Paul looked at him without saying a word and Peter, on a sudden impulse, asked the man a question that had haunted him for years. "Mr. Taggart, did you find me in a church once?"

Paul was startled. "Who told you that?"

"I heard a Sister say it once. I wasn't trying to hear what she was saying, Mr. Taggart. Honest, I wasn't." The boy's voice was shaking and he looked hopefully into Paul's eyes. "Did you find me, Mr. Taggart?"

Paul looked out over the fields and answered in a voice that was almost hoarse. "Yes, Peter. I found you."

Peter kept looking at him. This was the closest he had ever come to the mystery of his past and he wanted Mr. Taggart to tell him more. He had often wondered about himself. Sister Margaret evaded the question when he asked her about his parents. "Your father is dead, Peter," she had said long ago. "You will be a good boy and pray always for the repose of his soul." When he asked her about his mother, she smiled and told him to pray for her, too. She said it gently and firmly as if she were closing a book. Later, after Sister Margaret had gone back to New York, Peter knelt in the church and prayed for his father who was dead, and for his mother

· 73 ·

The Foundling

who was . . . "Where is she, God?" he had asked. "Who is my mother?"

Paul Taggart studied the boy as they sat there on the knoll that evening. "What's the trouble, Peter?"

"Nothing."

"Worrying about something?"

"Nope."

"Are you sure?"

Peter could not conceal the question any longer. "Mr. Taggart, who is my mother?"

Paul looked gravely at the boy and seemed to be deliberating before he answered. "Peter, I don't know who your mother is." He snuffed out his cigarette and continued, "But I can tell you this about your mother. She must have been beautiful and good."

"Beautiful and good?"

"Yes, Peter. She was beautiful and good enough to put you into a Christmas crib."

The boy looked at Mr. Taggart in doubt. "You're fooling me, Mr. Taggart."

"I'm not fooling you, Peter."

The sincerity in his voice aroused Peter and the boy raised himself quickly to his knees. "You mean my mother really put me in a Christmas crib?"

"Yes."

"Honest?"

Paul smiled. "Yes, Peter. That's where I found you. In a Christmas crib."

Peter looked out to where the west was all colored with

The Foundling

the sunset. For the first time in thirteen years he thought he saw his mother's face. It was out there somewhere beyond the pines and hills. Her face was a blend of all that was good and beautiful, a composite of all the kind looking women he had seen in books and magazines. His mother was young. She was poor. She was beautiful. It was all so very clear now. Because she was poor and beautiful and good, she had carried him into a church and left him in a crib to the care of the mother of Jesus.

"In a *real* Christmas crib, Mr. Taggart? Did she put me in a real one?"

"Yes, Peter. It was a real Christmas crib. She put you near the cows and donkey, and right next to Jesus and Mary."

Peter laughed. "And Saint Joseph, too?"

"And Saint Joseph, too."

Peter laughed again. He could have kissed Mr. Taggart, but he didn't because he was almost a man, being thirteen years old.

Peter was returning from the boulevard where Mr. Taggart had caught the bus to the Staten Island ferry when he spied Sister Crescentia, the pale, austere music teacher and organist of Mount Mary. With her was Theresa Bordano who had been left at the doors of the Foundling some thirteen years ago, blind at birth.

Peter slowed his steps so as not to overtake them. He was in awe of the tall nun, and as yet his associations with her had been confined to music instructions in classes, an occasional yea or a nay and the quickest possible exit. Now Sister

The Foundling

Crescentia beckoned to him, and when Peter reached her, she said, "I want you to take Theresa to the organ loft, Peter."

"Yes, Sister."

"I'll call for you shortly, Theresa," the nun added, hurrying off to St. John's.

The blind girl walked slowly by Peter's side. "What are you going to do in the organ loft, Theresa?" he asked.

"Practise," she answered.

He looked at her small, smiling face. "You play the organ, too, Theresa?"

"Yes, Peter." She wrinkled her nose. "I don't play so well, yet. It takes hours of practise."

"It must be hard when you can't see the notes."

"It is. If Sister Crescentia didn't spend so much time with me, I'd never learn."

"But how can you learn when you can't see?"

"It's my ear, and the feel of the board under my fingers."

"You mean you play everything by memory?"

"Yes. I *have* to, Peter."

The dark church was full of the fragrance of incense as they climbed the spiral stairs to the loft. After he unlocked the organ panels with the keys she had given him, Theresa turned to Peter and said, "Thanks, Peter. You may go now."

"I'd like to stay, Theresa. I'd like to hear you play."

"All right."

She laughed quietly and seated herself at the organ. In the twenty minutes that followed, this blind girl ran her fingers

The Foundling

deep into all Peter Lane's planning and gilded his dreams with glory.

He sat bent forward in the seat with his chin in his hands as the palest gleam of that dying September day slipped through a bit of open window. The music was exactly like that. It began under her fingers like a pale, cool light on far hills.

"What are you playing, Theresa?" he asked suddenly.

"Nothing yet," she answered. "I'm just feeling the organ."

For those twenty minutes during which she "felt" the organ, this blind girl played music that Peter had always wanted to hear. Peter's spirit echoed to the mood of the music. At first it was sombre. Then the organ brightened slowly. In the gathering darkness of the church the music glowed like so much sunlight coming back into the world. And Peter heard the crows and robins and bluebirds in it. Miraculously, and against the strictest rules of the school calendar, the birds were coming back again. They were sweeping about him in chattering clouds, telling him that summer was not done but would be endless. This blind girl with music-color flowing from her fingers painted the lovely picture for him.

He saw his silver silos gleaming in the distance. His two hundred cows were winding up out of the lowland mists; his thousand lambs were bleating in the meadows. All this was in Theresa's playing that evening. The longing to be out in the far fields where herds go lowing over the hills like drowsy silhouettes and crows go streaking homeward to the cool of the piney woods; the warm joy he had felt that evening on the knoll when Mr. Taggart had spoken about his mother—all this swept over thirteen-year-old Peter Lane again. Then he vowed to himself, "Someday it's going to be like this mother. Someday we'll be together and we'll be happy because I'll have silver silos and lime-washed barns. I'll have good, plowed fields for you, too. And orchards and vineyards. And I'll take you on a high seat in the surrey, behind Dan, and show you how fast he can run. We'll both be like the birds and we'll never have to go to school."

A foot on the spiral stairway aroused him. It was Chubby, his closest friend, the young Negro boy who had made himself a hero at Mount Mary by standing on his head a full five minutes (it was closer to two).

"I've been lookin' all over for you, Peter. What are you doin' up here?"

"Listening to music."

"Sounds good, huh?"

"Sounds swell. Do you like music, Chub?"

"I sure do. I like all kinds of music."

"Do you like organ music, Chub?"

"Organ, fiddle, harmonica, ukelele. It makes no difference to me. Just so long's it's music, I like it."

"Me too!"

Sister Crescentia entered the organ loft with a loud rattling of keys against her habit.

"I believe it's time both you boys were back in the recreation hall," she admonished.

"Yes, Sister," they agreed.

They both walked half way down the spiral stairs when Peter suddenly retraced his steps. Sister Crescentia was bending over the organ console with her fingers spread on the keys when he spoke.

"Sister Crescentia?"

"Yes, Peter?" The nun looked at him in surprise.

"Sister Crescentia, I want to play the organ like Theresa," Peter burst out.

"Me, too," Chubby blurted over Peter's shoulder.

"*You* want to play the organ?"

"Yes, Sister," they chanted.

She smiled faintly. "We'll see about that later," she said. "We'll see."

Chapter 10

It was soon common knowledge at Mount Mary that George (Chubby) Sands and Peter Lane had begun piano lessons. The nuns speculated on it; the farm hands discussed it; the boys joked about it; and the girls giggled over it.

Chubby pounded his way through monotonous schedules of scales. He lifted a weary head over the keyboard and sighed, "This stuff is awful, Peter. When do we start playin' for real on the organ?"

"We just got to be patient, Chub," Peter answered. "We'll be through in a little while."

"That's what I keep tellin' my fingers," Chubby mourned as he continued to practise into deeper and bluer boredom. "That's just what I keep tellin' these here fingers, Peter, but they just don't believe me anymore."

"Don't you like to practise scales, Chub?"

The Foundling

"Sure I like to practise scales, but I was all practised up twenty minutes ago. The trouble with piano lessons is you never stop when you're finished. The first thing you know these fingers are goin' to have a nervous breakdown."

"Maybe, if you tried to play a little slower, Chub, it wouldn't be so hard."

"Slower! That's just exactly what I'm trying to do. If I go any slower, I'll be backin' up into yesterday's lesson."

"Well, anyway it won't be long before we'll be playin' *Home Sweet Home*."

"Yeah," Chubby sighed sadly as he turned the pages of the exercise book. "But from the looks of these here pages, Peter, there's nothin' but a mess of misery between here and *Home Sweet Home*."

The days and weeks passed. Even the months passed. Then one morning, Chubby and Peter were summoned to Sister Crescentia's office.

"What do you think she wants, Chub?" Peter asked nervously.

"You got me. I didn't do anythin'." Chubby was quick in defense.

On the way to the office, they examined their respective consciences for any major or minor transgressions they might have committed in the past forty-eight hours. It couldn't be that they had failed to practise their music, for they had spent two hours at the piano the evening before. Indeed, for more than a year they had spent two hours daily in knuckle-breaking exercises at the piano, with three and a half hours on Sunday for good measure. And it couldn't have been that she had discovered them playing *Ida, Sweet as Apple Cider* when they should have been practicing Czerny. They never played *Ida, Sweet as Apple Cider* when Sister Crescentia was anywhere near Staten Island.

"Sit down, please," the nun began as soon as they had walked into the office.

They sat down and held their breath.

She began almost mysteriously. "A long time ago, both you boys told me you wanted to study music. Remember?"

"Yes, Sister," they whispered in awe.

"For a long time, I did not believe you were sincere," she said, lifting a large cloth-bound ledger from a shelf. "But now, boys, I want to excuse myself."

Peter and Chubby were startled at this strange turn in the conversation.

Sister Crescentia turned the pages of her large enrollment book, and her eyes strayed from Peter to Chubby. "How old are you, George?"

"Fourteen, Sister."

"And you, Peter?"

"Fifteen."

She nodded slowly as if weighing something in her mind. "You're men enough to take a little bit of praise, aren't you?" And before Chubby could assure her that they were, she continued, "In less than two years you both mastered Hanon and Cramer."

This was a veritable benediction coming from Sister Crescentia, for not once in all the time they had studied piano had she ever praised them.

"In my seventeen years of teaching music, there was only one boy who did that."

Peter and Chubby glowed visibly under her approval.

She consulted the schedule in her enrollment ledger again and added: "I am amazed that in such a short time you can also play that little book of preludes by Bach."

"And yesterday, I waited outside the pavilion and heard your *Für Elise*."

"We wanted to try Beethoven, Sister," Chubby explained, knowing how strenuously she objected to anything outside the regular assignments.

Sister Crescentia smiled. "I was proud of you boys yesterday. You took the arpeggios with feathers in your fingers."

Feathers in their fingers! How many nights and how many days they had tried, for her sake, to put feathers in their fingers. How many weary winter afternoons and summer mornings they had rehearsed the rapid finger climbing. Their wrists had ached and the monotony of it had almost driven Chubby mad. How many times had he felt the necessity to jump off his stool and walk about the room, trying to shake the terrible regularity of it from his brain and joints. "Your arpeggios are neither rhythmic nor in tempo," she had criticized them during those afternoons. "You boys are running up a flight of stairs and your thumbs are kicking every landing. Put feathers in; put feathers in your fingers, boys!" That was how she had spoken last February.

So now at last they had feathers in their fingers. Under the spell of her enthusiasm, and knowing how much she revered Chopin, Chubby hastened to add another star to his already blazing firmament. "We have even been experimenting with Chopin's *B Minor Prelude,* Sister!"

She stared meditatively at the Negro boy and then closed the book. "I had a special reason for wanting to see you two this morning." She walked to the front of the desk and folded her arms. "Tomorrow is Sunday. It's going to be a nice day, and I believe you boys deserve an outing. New York City is beautiful on a Sunday afternoon." She was still standing there imperiously, with folded arms, when she added, "Tell Sister Felicia that you have my permission to go to New York and ask her, please, to give you three dollars." Then she dismissed them.

It was so like Sister Crescentia, Chubby and Peter agreed on the way back to the dormitory. "She makes no fuss at all, does she, Peter? She just ups and gives you an outin' just like she jugs you."

"She's a square shooter, isn't she, Chub?"

"She sure is. I never saw a Sister I was so scared of and that I liked so much all at the same time."

When they approached the dormitory, Chubby suddenly stopped and snapped his fingers. "I just thought of somethin', Peter. Somethin' wonderful about tomorrow when we go to New York."

"What is it?"

The Negro boy faced Peter. He was about to speak, but his face turned curiously grave. "I guess it's nothin' special, Peter. It's just maybe nothin'," he faltered.

Peter knew Chubby was worried.

"Maybe someday I'll tell you, Peter."

"Tell me what?"

"Some day I'll tell you about somethin'. It's a secret."

Peter wondered how long he would have to wait before Chubby would tell him the secret. Maybe weeks, months. Maybe years. Maybe even forever. People sometimes forgot to tell you their special secrets.

That afternoon at dinner Chubby leaned over and whispered to Peter, "Know what, Peter?"

"What?"

"I'm goin' to tell you that secret this afternoon!"

"Okay, Chub."

"Up at the mound. Okay?"

"Okay."

"I'm goin' to tell it to you, Peter, because you're my best friend."

"You're my best friend, too, Chub."

"Am I, Peter? You haven't got a better friend than me, have you?"

Peter was instantly lost in thought—in a juggling of friendship values. There was Mr. Paul Taggart, of course. He was like his own father. He was good, and strong, and manly. And Mrs. Taggart, too. She was part of Paul. Then there was Sister Margaret, and she was almost like your own mother. There was also little fourteen-year-old Theresa Bordano, the blind girl at Saint Mary's. He was sure he loved Theresa because she had a nice face, and because she was blind. Theresa was more like a sweetheart than anything else.

"We'll always be the two best friends in the world, won't we, Peter?" Chubby continued.

The Foundling

"We sure will, Chub. No other friends will be better friends than us two."

"Shake!"

They shook on it.

When they reached the mound that afternoon, Chubby removed a soiled envelope from his pocket. "This is my special secret, Peter. Here, read this letter."

Peter unfolded the paper and read the simple message that had been written in pencil.

"Dear George,

"Jean is back from the hospital, she came back last week and she is staying with me. You asked me to write to you when she came back from the hospital and I am writing to you so you know. Jean is not feeling so good but she looks much better and she feels better. But maybe you better not see her right away because I think it is too soon to see her yet. I will write again and let you know about how she is. Did you receive the rock candy and the tie? Good-by George. . . . Noella Anderson."

Peter folded the letter and returned it to Chubby. "Who is Jean?"

"Jean is my sister, Peter." Chubby said it almost in a whisper.

"Sister! I didn't know you had a sister."

"I didn't know it either until maybe two months ago. Mrs. Anderson told me never to say anythin' about it."

"How does Mrs. Anderson know Jean is your sister?"

"She told me. She knows all about Jean. She's a nice lady,

Mrs. Anderson is, she visits me often and when she first told me about Jean, do you know what she said?"

"What?"

"She said, 'George, I'm goin' to tell you somethin' because you're gettin' old, and it's somethin' you ought to know.' Then she told me about Jean. She said Jean is my sister, and that she was sick for years and years."

"What was the matter with Jean?"

"I don't know. She was just sick, that's all. Mrs. Anderson said everybody thought Jean would die, and that it would be no good to ever tell me I had a sister if she was goin' to die. But now that Jean ain't goin' to die, Mrs. Anderson thought she better tell me about her. See?"

Chubby was stumbling over himself in his efforts to make it all clear.

"How old is Jean, Chub?"

"I don't know."

Peter lay back on the mound and looked upwards at Chubby. "Boy, it must be nice to have a real sister."

The eyes of the Negro boy were dancing. "You bet it's nice, Peter, especially when you always thought you never had nobody." He lay back in the grass and his dark face was turned to the sky. "Yeah, I got me a real live sister, Peter. I guess I'm the luckiest guy at Mount Mary." A few seconds later, Chubby lifted himself quickly on his elbows. He was staring intently at Peter. "Know what I'm goin' to do tomorrow, Peter?"

"What?"

"I'm goin' to see her!" Chubby almost recoiled at having

blurted this secret to Peter. It was against the rules and regulations to visit without permission. He looked hungrily at Peter. "It's my first chance to see Jean. I want to . . . sort of surprise her."

"That's a swell idea," Peter breathed.

Chubby bent close to Peter. "You'll come with me, won't you, Peter?"

"Sure I will, Chub."

"And we won't tell Sister Crescentia or anybody, okay?"

"Okay."

Chubby's clean laughter rang in the afternoon. He was totally happy; and then in the next instant his face clouded. "Peter," he hedged, "you know my pants, the gray ones?"

"Yeah."

"Well, they're just a bit busted in the left knee. You can't really see my knee unless you look hard, but I was wonderin' if . . ."

"You can wear my pants, Chub. We'll switch."

"Gee, you're my best friend all right, Peter."

"They won't notice my knee as quick as they'll see yours, Chub, on account of my skin is white."

Chubby laughed. "That's right, Peter. When you got black skin like I got, you sure bust through all that light-colored stuff."

So that was arranged, readily and simply.

"You can have my tie with the yellow dots, too, Chub."

"Man, that's a tie what's a tie," Chubby exploded. "Wait'll Jean sees me!" He relaxed again and dreamed about this first meeting with his sister. "She's goin' to be some surprised when I knock at the door and say, 'Hello, Jean. It's me. Your brother Georgie.' Boy, is she goin' to be surprised! And then . . . maybe . . . she'll sort of kiss me and laugh. Sisters do that to you, Peter?"

"Sisters practically do everything, Chub."

"Boy, I'm lucky. I think I won't sleep at all tonight thinkin' about Jean." Chubby sighed contentedly. As an afterthought, he added: "You don't think she'll be mad at me for comin' without tellin' her, do you, Peter?"

"Nah. Jean'll like it."

"Sure she'll like it," Chubby agreed. "She was in the hospital for years and years, and now the best thing for her is to see me, her own brother. Right, Peter?"

"Right, Chub."

Chapter 11

On the following day Peter Lane and Chubby Sands set out on their quest for Jean. Two hours after they had landed in New York City, they stood dubiously outside a narrow tenement off Eighth Avenue.

"Is this the house, Chub?"

"It's the house, all right. It says so right here on this letter."

The janitor was standing in the doorway. "What do you boys want?" he asked.

"Does Noella Anderson live here?"

"Three flights up in the back," the man directed.

Peter had a difficult time keeping up with Chubby, who was taking the stairs two at a time. They finally reached a door marked N. Anderson.

Chubby hesitated. "Suppose nobody's at home."

"They'll be home, Chub. Don't worry."

The Foundling

While they were speaking, the door opened slowly. A frail Negro girl in a faded pink dress faced them. "You looking for somebody?"

"I'm lookin' for Mrs. Noella Anderson," Chubby began.

"She lives here," the girl answered. "But Noella is out right now."

Chubby stared fixedly at the girl. She appeared to be about seventeen or eighteen years old. When he spoke, his voice was frightened. "Are you . . . are you Jean?"

"No. My name's Mimi. Jean is gone away but she'll come back."

Chubby was crestfallen.

"Go ahead, Chub," Peter whispered. "Tell her who you are."

"I'm George Sands," Chubby began weakly.

"George?"

"Jean's brother."

The girl seemed to be looking past Chubby. Her face was expressionless. Water was running in a sink somewhere and she tilted her head to listen. Then she said emptily, "They didn't tell me you were coming. They never tell me anything, anymore."

"Where's Jean now?" Chubby asked.

"She went away but she'll come back soon."

"I'd like to see her today," Chubby continued. "If you could tell me where to find her, I could go and . . ."

"What is your name again?" she interrupted.

"George Sands."

The girl was studying Chubby closely. Then she smiled

· 91 ·

The Foundling

slowly, and in that flashing instant Peter thought she was pretty. Her eyes, lustrous-dark, were clear and cool; and to look at her skin was to remember good earth that had been turned and tanned in the sun. The loose pink dress, fastened at her throat by a broken button, fell in folds almost to her feet. But when you looked at her face, you forgot the dress and the broken button.

Again her face was expressionless when she spoke. "Come in, won't you? You mustn't stand in the hall. It's so nice inside, and I want to speak to you."

She led them into a small room. It was a very dark room. Sunlight barely seeped through a window that was thrust against a damp, red, brick wall. Three chairs, a table and a narrow bed were the simple furnishings. A large cardboard box, lying in a corner, was half-filled with artificial red roses. Strands of wire wrapped in green wax-paper were scattered on the floor near the box.

The girl sat near the flowers and looked at Peter. "It is such a long time without seeing someone. They never come to hear me sing anymore."

Chubby was puzzled. "Sing? Do you sing?"

"I used to sing. Everybody used to come and hear me sing. Mr. Sam stood near the window when I sang and he never went away." Her face was tired and her eyes were distant again. "Mr. Sam always brought the flowers and the small boxes. He said that I could sing better than anybody in the world. That's why I sang for Mr. Sam. He always used to stand by the window and say, 'Mimi, sing old Sammy's song.' That's why I sang for Mr. Sam. I also sang

The Foundling

for the flowers and the small boxes. The flowers and the small boxes are pretty. Do you want me to sing for the flowers and boxes?"

Peter felt a sudden chill in the room. There was something odd, something vague and mysterious about this girl, Mimi. He looked at Chubby and saw his fingers twitching at his knees.

"The flowers and the small boxes?" Chubby asked.

"The pretty flowers and boxes," she repeated. She was smiling again. "I want to have the flowers and boxes near me. Mr. Sam brings them and he takes them away."

Chubby turned wide eyes at Peter.

"Do you feel sick, Mimi?" Peter asked fearfully.

"Noella keeps saying I'm sick, but Mr. Sam says I'm not sick. He always brings the flowers back and forth out of the room and then he goes away."

Peter suspected then that the girl was out of her mind, and when she looked at him he felt he had to say something. "Mimi, do you make flowers?"

"Yes, I make flowers. See them!" She indicated the large box in the corner. "See the flowers." Her face was suddenly happy. "You can have the flowers and boxes. Take them to Mr. Sam and bring him back." She bent and lifted one of the roses. Holding it under her chin, she unconsciously struck a pretty picture. Sitting forward in the chair, and gazing upwards at the ceiling, her eyes were lost in rapture. Then her lips parted; a quick flicker of joy passed over her face, and the room went suddenly ringing with the singing of her voice. "*Si. Mi chiamano Mimi* . . ." she sang, and as her voice

The Foundling

soared to strange and haunting strength Peter turned and faced Chubby. The Negro boy was standing.

"Maybe we'd better get out of here, Chub. Maybe we'd better come back later."

The hall door opened at that instant, and an old Negro woman entered. She stopped in surprise when she saw Peter and Chubby. "Excuse me, I didn't know you were here." The woman's voice was barely audible above the singing. "Is Mrs. Anderson around?"

"Mrs. Anderson is out," Peter answered.

"It's a shame the way Noella leaves this girl all alone like this."

The woman bent over the singing girl who seemed totally unconscious of her presence.

"What's the matter with her?" Peter asked.

"She's . . . she's just sick, that's all." The woman was purring easily. "You'll be all right in a little while, Jean. You hear me, Jean baby?"

Jean!

Peter looked at Chubby. "It's Jean, Chub," he whispered. "It's your sister."

Chubby's face was cold, taut. Only his lips moved. He tried to say something and then covered his mouth with his hands.

"She's sick, Chub. Jean's just plain sick," Peter tried to comfort him.

"She don't know me," Chubby whimpered. "She's never goin' to know that I'm her brother."

"She likes to sing about the flowers," the woman explained, stroking the hair of the girl. "That's why she keeps singing. Night and day she sings ole Sam's song, poor child."

"Don't worry, Chub. She'll be all right," Peter added lamely.

"She don't know me," Chubby repeated in a stupor.

"You just go on and sing if you want to, honey child," the woman soothed. "You just keep singing ole Sam Cooper's song, 'cause you got the beautifullest voice in the whole world. Yes, you have." The woman was kneeling at Jean's feet, and her large arm encircled the slim waist of the girl. "You sing all you want to, honey, and tell ole Henrietta about Mr. Sam and the flowers."

"*Sola mi fo il pranzo da me stessa . . .*" Jean's voice was plaintive and soft now.

"Go on, Jean baby, and tell ole Henrietta about all the little flowers."

"*Non vado sempre a messa . . .*"

"You're so full of misery, child." The old woman was chanting her words, and her eyes were wet.

"*Vivo sola, soletta . . .*"

"You're going to be happy, child. The good Lord, He's going to take care of you. Yes, He will."

"*Ma quando vien lo sgelo il primo sole e mio . . .*" Jean's voice was alive now with a vibrant ecstasy of tone.

The woman sobbed. "You going to be all right, Jean. You going to have all the flowers in the world. Yes, you will, child. There's going to be nothing but daisies and daffydills for Jeannie. All the nice roses and carnations that you don't

The Foundling

have to make with your hands, child. God's just going to throw them 'round your feet, Jean baby. Yes, He will."

When the song was ended, Jean sank back against the chair.

"You feel better now, Jean?" the woman asked.

Jean stared happily into space for a moment. Then she said, "Where's Noella?"

"She'll be right back, honey. Now, you set there and ole Henrietta's going to make you a cup of coffee." The woman rose to her feet and faced Peter and Chubby. "How come you folks are visiting with Jean?"

"I'm her brother," Chubby explained simply.

"Her brother!" The woman was visibly surprised. "You mean you're Jean's brother?" She broke off abruptly and a glimmer of recognition crept slowly into her face.

But Chubby was not listening to the woman. He walked to the chair on which Jean sat. "Jean, I'm George. I'm your brother."

The girl was smiling at Chubby.

"You understand me, Jean?" Chubby reached for her hand. "I'm your real brother. Look at me."

The room was tense.

Chubby was whimpering under her blank stare.

Then Jean sighed wearily and asked, "Where's Noella?"

"You see, it don't do no good," the old woman said, shaking her head sorrowfully. "She's sick, Jean is. All she's good for is singing and making flowers."

"How long has she been like this?" Chubby asked.

"Long as I can remember. Years and years. She goes away

to the hospital, and she comes back, and it don't do no good."

"Why does she sing like that?"

"'Cause singing is what she likes to do. Singing and making flowers. Sam, ole Sam Cooper who lives upstairs, he's the one who taught her how to sing and make the flowers. I guess that old Jewish man's about the best friend she got in this world. Sam and Noella. And maybe me."

Chubby was staring at Jean whose eyes were closed. She appeared to be dozing.

"C'mon, son. You just sit down and make yourself comfortable. Henrietta's going to fix us all some coffee."

"No, thanks," Chubby said. "I think I'd better leave now." He moved quickly to the door, and when he was out in the hall, Peter saw him shiver.

"I want to see you a minute, son," Henrietta called to Chubby. "I want to talk to you alone."

Chubby hesitated. "What do you want?"

"Come in here. Got something to tell you."

"I'll wait outside," Peter said, moving to the door.

For at least a half hour he waited, and when Chubby finally opened the door, Peter noticed that his face was like a tight mask with pain.

"Don't worry about Jean, Chub," Peter tried to be encouraging as they descended the stairs.

But Chubby was silent.

Twenty minutes later, they were riding on the subway. The express roared southward through the tunnel. It was a noisy, exciting world down here in the subway, full of the

The Foundling

rumble of thundering wheels and the blue flicker of electric flame. By rights, it should have been a bright world. The posters advertising gloves, shampoo, medicine, and mustard were brilliant behind the row of burning electric bulbs. Even the people were dressed colorfully on this Sunday afternoon. But Peter was looking at the window opposite. In it, he saw the reflection of Chubby's face, murky, grayish, and distorted in the dirty glass. Chubby looked like an old man, Peter thought.

"What are we going to do, Chub?" Peter asked.

"I don't know. You said something about the Museum of Natural History."

Peter frowned, deliberated. "Would you like to go there?"

"Makes no difference to me."

"How about Central Park. There may be a game there."

"Anywhere."

"Or do you want to see a movie?"

Chubby breathed heavily. "It's all the same to me, Peter."

"You're not sick or anything, are you?"

"No. I'm all right. Honest."

"Would you like to call on the Taggarts?"

"If you want to, Peter, but I sort of don't want to see anyone. Just let's go somewhere, just us."

The rest of the day went by slowly. It had all the makings of a holiday—a movie, a walk across Forty-second Street, a dinner in a small restaurant, the trip to South Ferry, and then the last lap to Mount Mary. But through it all, Peter felt the growing dejection in Chubby.

The Foundling

That night, Peter whispered from his bed, "Don't worry about Jean, Chub. She's going to be all right."

There was a slight pause before Chubby answered. "Peter, what would you do, if you had a sister like Jean?"

"I don't know. I never thought about it."

A long silence followed. Then Chubby whispered, "You and I are the best friends in the world, Peter. Right?"

"Right."

"Shake on it."

"Shake, Chub."

They leaned from their beds and gripped each other by the hand. It was an old game. They had repeated this pledge many times. Tonight, Peter thought, Chubby's grip was tighter than it had ever been before.

They lay back in bed then.

"Some day, Peter, I'm going to tell you another secret. It's a secret nobody knows, not even Sister Crescentia."

"Nobody knows it?"

"Nobody knows it 'cepting God and me and somebody else."

"All right, Chub. I'll wait till you tell me."

They were very quiet then, locked apart in separate worlds of meditation.

Chapter 12

ON THE following afternoon, old Father Duane, rector of Mount Mary, lifted his pen over the open book. He wondered for a moment how the record for the day should be worded. It had been a most unusual and confusing sort of day, beginning, of course, with that knock on the door that morning.

"Come in," he had invited.

"I want to see you, Father." It was Chubby Sands.

"Yes, George, what can I do for you?"

"I came to say good-by."

"Where are you going?"

"I'm running away."

It had struck him as a unique announcement. "That's interesting, George. Have you packed all your clothes?"

"Yes, Father."

"And you know the proper gate to sneak through?" The

The Foundling

irony was calculated to bring the boy back to his senses.

"I'm not going through the gate. I'm going over the wall."

"I see. And I'm sure you have informed Sister Crescentia."

"No, Father. She wouldn't understand."

"And what do you want me to do? Give you my blessing?"

"No, I just came to say good-by."

He had studied the boy closely at this point. "Now please tell me what on earth is on your mind, George."

The story had unfolded then in quick, matter-of-fact phrases. When Chubby had concluded, his features were grim.

Father Duane asked quietly, "What makes you think you can help your sister, George?"

"I can work. I can do a lot of things."

"But I forbid you to leave."

"You can't forbid me."

This had been a shocking blow to his clerical authority. "Why can't I forbid you?"

"Because . . . because God won't like it, that's why."

"But you know the regulations. You're not eligible for release."

"I don't care about the regulations, Father. All I know is I got a sister and she needs me. There isn't anybody who can stop me. You could even lock me up, but I'd still run away somehow."

"I see."

"So I came to say good-by."

There had been one last stab at formality, one last fling

The Foundling

at righteousness. "George, won't you change your mind for my sake? Can't you see I'm trying to help you?"

"I know you're trying to help me, but I got all the help I need. I owe everything I got to you and the Sisters. Maybe some day I'll be able to pay you back. It's Jean who needs the help now."

It had been just like that—thrust and counter-thrust. The inflexible will of this Negro boy was written in clean, hard lines along his jaw.

"All right, George. I see what you mean. But can't you wait for a few days? You've got to give us more time."

"I'm sorry, Father." His lip had trembled then. "I can't wait. I can't stop thinking about Jean. Good-by, Father."

"Wait a minute," he interrupted, as Chubby turned to leave. It took a few sober moments to come to the decision. "There's a tin box in my desk. I want you to open it."

Chubby moved slowly to the desk and lifted the lid of the box.

"How much money is in there?"

Chubby counted it slowly. "Thirty-six dollars."

"Money is an important item in life, George. You'll find it comes in handy."

"I guess it does, Father."

"You will need that thirty-six dollars."

Chubby tried gallantly to refuse. "I can't take it. Honest."

"I didn't give you permission to take it. I said merely you'll need that thirty-six dollars."

"Thanks, Father."

"And now I presume you will stay with Mrs. Anderson."

The Foundling

The Negro boy had looked sharply, suspiciously at him. "I don't know."

"You will get to like Mrs. Anderson." Then he had measured the words slowly, emphatically, "I want you to like Mrs. Anderson, George."

Chubby's eyes were black, brooding, questioning. "Maybe there won't be room for me and Jean both."

"I'm sure Mrs. Anderson will make room. I'll contact the Welfare Board tomorrow."

Then he had handed the boy an address. "Go and see Mr. Hatson. He'll help you, George."

"Thanks, Father."

"Don't thank me. Remember, I didn't give you permission to leave these grounds."

When the boy had reached the door, he had one further suggestion to add. "George, you know that back wall you're going to sneak over?"

"Yes, Father."

"It's a little out of the way. I suggest you go out the main gate."

"But one of the Sisters might stop me."

"Nobody will stop you, George. That's the way you came in, and that's the way you're going out. The main gate at three o'clock, this afternoon."

"I see. The main gate at three o'clock this afternoon," he repeated. Then he smiled and held out his hand. "Good-by, Father."

"Good-by, George, and God bless you."

Two minutes later, Father Duane had picked up the house

The Foundling

phone and called Sister Crescentia. "I want to inform you that George Sands is leaving for New York this afternoon."

There was an audible gasp. "Leaving Mount Mary?"

"Yes."

"But, Father, we've made no arrangements. We haven't consulted . . ."

"Arrangements aren't necessary, Sister. He's made up his mind to leave."

"We must put a stop to it immediately," the nun said with determination.

"I wouldn't if I were you, Sister."

"But the Welfare Board, and the . . ."

"I'll take care of the Welfare Board, Sister. Right now, there is only one thing I'd like you to do."

"Yes, Father." Sister Crescentia's voice was a wavering compromise between rebellion and acquiescence.

"I want you to give George a lift to the ferry. Put him on the four o'clock boat." And before the bewildered nun could add an objection, he had hung up.

There had only been one further detail to attend to, and that was a rush telegram to Noella Anderson. "Meet George at St. George. Boat at four o'clock," the message read.

"That ought to do it," Father Duane breathed, filling his pipe that afternoon. "That surely ought to do it."

So the pen was poised now over the page. It was almost four o'clock. Chubby had gone out the front gate at three o'clock, with a swarm of nuns, including Sister Crescentia, in the community beach wagon.

"That ferry is just about getting ready to pull out of the

slip," Father Duane muttered to himself as he dipped the pen in the ink. Then he smiled and wrote the words laboriously across the page:

"George Sands (son of Noella Anderson Sands) went home today. Arranged for immediate release this afternoon. $36.00 Ad Majorem Dei Gloriam. May God be with you through all the nights and days, Chub."

Chapter 13

GEORGE SANDS, Negro, fourteen years old, one hundred and thirty-two pounds, sat in the smoking cabin of the Staten Island ferry. A small suitcase, salvaged from the cedar closets of Mount Mary in the hurried preparations for his quick departure, was lying at his feet. Thirty-six dollars, one extra suit in his valise, and a small stack of mail, mostly postcards, was the exact sum of physical assets he could muster as he faced the world. Never in all his life had Chubby felt so rich, so secure. *Thirty-six dollars!*

Yet Chubby Sands was not happy. He was trying to think. He was trying to put all his fourteen-year-old thoughts into some kind of order. Ever since yesterday when Henrietta told him that Mrs. Anderson was his mother, his thoughts were mixed. It was a secret, Henrietta had said. He had refused at first to believe Henrietta. "If Mrs. Anderson is my mother, why didn't she tell me?" He had asked the question fiercely. But the old woman had persisted. "You got to know it some day, son. Mrs. Anderson is going to tell you herself. Yes, she will."

So it was a secret. It was his mother's secret; and now it was also his secret.

Chubby began talking to himself.

Sitting there in the ferry, it made him dizzy to think about what had happened and what to do about it. He tried to untangle all his thoughts, but they wouldn't untangle. They were full of knots, full of tight, bulging knots like the knots one sees on packages. Every knot was a question, and every question was the same. What was the secret? Why didn't his mother tell him she was his mother? He tried to pick the knots apart with his thinking. But the knots were too tight.

Sitting there in the ferry, he began to think about yesterday all over again. It was like a dream. In a way he wished it was a dream. He could wake up and forget Jean. He could walk along the road with Peter and some of his other friends and say, "Boy, what a nightmare I had last night. I dreamed I had a crazy sister." But it wasn't a dream, and he almost cried to think that he had a crazy sister. Only he would never say that word "crazy" to anybody. It was an ugly word. His sister was sick, that's all. And he loved her even more because she was that way.

Sitting there in the ferry, the knots were still raveled in his head. It was getting worse in a way. Everything was getting more jumbled and scarey. But he wasn't really scared. He knew what he was going to do. He was going to work for Jean. He would work hard and bring her back real money like the thirty-six dollars he had in his pocket. He would buy

The Foundling

her lamb chops, and steaks, and milk, and he would sit near her and watch her eat and see her get well and strong. He'd spend the rest of his life for Jean because she was his sister. He didn't like the roses she was making. He would tell her to forget the roses and come out of that dark room. He would take her for nice long walks in the park and bring her to movies and treat her to banana splits and coffee cake. Nobody in New York City would ever think there was anything wrong with Jean when he was out walking with her. They would say, "There goes Jean with her brother, George." Then maybe God, plus all the money he would make, plus the walks and talks in the park would stop Jean from making roses and singing. She would be nice and normal and not "sick" anymore.

But sitting there in the ferry, the knots kept coming back and rubbing inside his head. The boat was moving now. He was going away forever from the Mount. It was good-by to the Sisters, to his friends and most especially to Peter. He liked Peter better than anybody in the world, he told himself, anybody except Jean. He didn't know whether he loved his mother or not, because the knots were still in his thinking. It was funny to think that Mrs. Anderson could be his real, actual mother. He recalled her face. It was a kind face but it was a worried face, too. It was the face he had expected to see on visiting Sundays only. He was grateful that she came on visiting Sundays. He always thanked her for the candy she brought in brown bags. He laughed and talked with her, but somehow he always ran out of talk after the first half hour. He got uncomfortable because it seemed that,

The Foundling

after the first half hour, Mrs. Anderson would always get too quiet. She was always looking closely at him. She was always about to say something, and then she would say nothing. Maybe she was thinking about the secret on those visiting Sundays. Maybe she was looking at him and wondering if she should tell him the secret. Maybe if she had come right out and said, "I'm your mother, George," maybe if she had come right out and said it like that, it wouldn't be so bad. But she had never said it, and so the knots in his head were tight and hard as ever.

Sitting there in the ferry, he wished he could go to sleep and forget. He closed his eyes. His head was tired with all the thinking. It was really like a dream. His world was spinning now in a dizzy whirl of tenements, subways, stairs, chairs, and girls who were singing in tangles of red roses. His mind went tumbling back over a maze of memories, of days gone by, of lights and shadows, and sounds; back to half remembered hungerings for someone or something; back through boyhood, through schooldays and music lessons, memories of teachers and playmates, orchards and fields, baseball and football, skating and coasting, kites and marbles. Far back and back he went until his memory was lost in the gray babble of small dormitories, in childish fears and littleness, to days beyond memory; back, back to a blank wall . . . and a question mark.

Chubby Sands was sitting there on the ferry with his eyes closed when the woman sat down beside him.

"I've been looking all over the boat for you, George."

The Foundling

It was his mother.

The boy shrank slightly and stared at Noella. "How did you know I was leaving?"

"I got a telegram." She fumbled in her pocketbook for a handkerchief and wiped beads of perspiration from her forehead. "I knew you would come anyway, George. Henrietta told me about yesterday." Her lips were moving strangely, as if she were trying to fight back something. "You know everything, now, George."

"Why didn't you tell me you were my mother?" Chubby's eyes were dark and accusing.

"I'll tell you. It really started this way. You're going to know it from beginning to end." She took a deep breath and began to pour out the story she had been wanting for years to tell. "It was a Tuesday night, and . . ."

George could almost see the subway and the people in it that Tuesday night fourteen years ago, as his mother described the tragedy of their lives. Chubby lived the tragedy as his mother re-lived it in telling it to her son.

The big Negro was standing there in the subway holding the black tin lunch kit under his arm. The big Negro was George. He was your father. George Sands. He was a strong man. He had to be a strong man because he was a sandhog. Sandhogs, the way your mother described them, sandhogs were men who worked in tunnels under a river. They worked in compressed air. You had to be strong to work in compressed air. So you sat there on the ferry and felt the first faint stirring of something great in your heart. Your father was a strong sandhog and he made good pay. Steady pay. He made enough pay to take care of Jean who was only four years old. Jean was sick in her head. Ever since she was born, she was like that. But your father loved Jean. He would take her gently in his strong arms—your mother was crying softly when she said this, and he would sing cute little songs to her. He sang songs to her every night up to that terrible Tuesday night. That Tuesday night, everything began to be different.

So anyway, your father was standing there in the subway with his lunch kit under his arm, when the men came into the train at Eighty-sixth Street. There were two of them. It was clear the way your mother explained it. You saw your father walk to the empty seat and sit in it. Then you heard one of the men who came on at Eighty-sixth Street shout. He said something like this at first. "Get out of that seat, nigger." It was something like that. Your mother wasn't sure what the man had said because your father himself had never been too sure about it, either. But anyway, the man told your father to get out of the seat, and your father said something like this. "Who's going to make me get out of this seat?" He said it in a loud booming voice, because your mother told you he had a big voice, and he was never afraid to use it. So, one of the men walked very close to your father and bent over him. Then he said the words that the woman riding on the subway, Mrs. Phillips, heard. Mrs. Phillips heard the words because she put her hand on the Bible in the court two weeks later, and she swore to tell the whole truth and nothing but the truth so help her, God. Mrs.

The Foundling

Phillips said she was sitting right next to your father and she heard the man say, "If you don't get out of that seat, nigger, I'll throw you out of it." Mrs. Phillips said she could smell whiskey or beer on the man's breath. Anyway, that's what the man said to your father. So your father got out of the seat and with his loud voice he said, "What did you call me, mister?" Then nobody knows for sure what happened after that because there was a fight on the train, and women screamed. Some people grabbed your father and some people grabbed the man.

It might have stopped there, your mother said. It all might have ended there, but it didn't. The two men followed your father out of the train at One Hundred Twenty-fifth Street. Then they began fighting in the station. Mrs. Phillips who got off the train at One Hundred Twenty-fifth Street saw what happened. She saw the men push your father against the wall and start to beat him. But your father was strong, and to listen to your mother tell you about it, you felt a kind of wild glory running in your blood. Your father was beating the men all by himself. That's how strong your father was. Then the cops came. They took your father and the two men to the station house.

Your mother was looking closely at you now with her large brown eyes and she asked you if you were understanding all the things she was saying. You told her you understood.

So she continued. She said it might have ended there, but it didn't. The men wanted a trial. They were out to get your father. So the trial came. The judge was a nice man. The judge listened to Mrs. Phillips. He listened to your father and to the two men. Then the judge said something like this. "You two men are a menace to society. I declare George Sands innocent. You deliberately provoked a law-abiding citizen to violence." Your mother said the words as if she had been repeating them all her life. The judge also fined the two men. He was a good judge, your mother said.

It might have stopped there too, your mother said. It might have been forgotten, but it wasn't. Two weeks later, when your father was coming home from the tunnels with his lunch kit, three men stopped him in the hall. It was the hall of the house where we lived. One of the three men said something to your father, which your father repeated in the trial six months later. The man said, "This will teach you to know your place, nigger." That was what one of the three men said to your father. Your father remembered nothing after that except the face of the man who struck him over the head. Then everything went black for your father. Your mother heard the neighbors screaming in the hall. Your mother went down the stairs and found your father lying in a pool of blood. A half hour later, your father opened his eyes in Mrs. Someone's flat. Your mother didn't remember the neighbor's name. But they carried your father into Mrs. Someone's flat because he was too heavy to carry up four flights of stairs. Your father opened his eyes and he said, "Where are they?"

Then he said to someone, "Give me a drink." So they gave your father a drink. It was whiskey he wanted, because when your father said "give me a drink" like that, he meant

The Foundling

he wanted whiskey. Your father had six or seven drinks. His face was cut, and his eyes were swelled up where the men hit him. Then your father got off the couch and he said, "I'll be back later, woman." Your mother said she tried to stop him, but it was no use. When your father wanted to do something, he did it. So your father went out that night.

Your mother was breathing hard now. She sat more close to you on the ferry boat, and you could judge from the way her mouth was twisting that she was going to tell you something important. She said your father went out that night and never came back to the house again. She was crying now, and the man who was reading the newspaper on the seat opposite looked up. You wished she wouldn't cry like that because people aren't supposed to cry on ferry boats. But you didn't mind too much, either, because you figured it meant a lot to your mother.

So she continued. She said that when your father left the house that night, he went to a barber shop where he got a gun. Then he got into a taxi and rode to an athletic club downtown. The taxi man said that he remembered your father telling him to drive as fast as he could to that athletic club. So he drove there fast. Then your father got out of the taxi and waited outside a bakery. The bakery was right next to the athletic club. He waited for five or six minutes and then a car pulled up outside the athletic club. Three men got out of the car. They walked to the athletic club, but before they reached the door, your father stopped them.

Your mother was looking very close at you now and she said this is what you got to believe. Your father told it to her, and your father was an honest man. Your father wasn't a drinking man. He was quiet and respectable. He wouldn't hurt a fly . . . your father wouldn't.

"See, George?"

Chubby nodded.

So your mother said your father shouted out loud in the street that night. Outside the athletic club, he said to the three men, "Somebody hired you to get me. Somebody inside." The men told your father to get out of the way. But your father said, "There're two men inside who hired you to get me." Then the three men tried to knock your father down, but your father wouldn't go down. Your mother's lips were tight when she said that. She said you got to know it all, George. You got to know everything now. You got to remember that your father was drinking that night, and that maybe it wasn't his fault. When you're drinking, you don't know what you're doing, sometimes. That's what your mother said.

So she continued.

She said your father shook the three men off him. Then he went inside the athletic club. He found the two men he was looking for—the two men who tried to beat him up on the train, the two men who lived in the club as your father learned in court when the judge fined them. He didn't say anything to these men.

Your mother was squeezing your arm and crying for real, now.

She said your father stood in front of the two men he was looking for. He didn't say anything to them. He just

The Foundling

shot them. One man died in the athletic club. The other man didn't die. The other man went to the hospital.

Later your father had a trial. The judge was sorry. But he was strict, too. The judge said your father was sentenced to prison from forty years to life. Some people said your father should have been electrocuted. He was guilty of murder. So, some people said he should have been electrocuted. But other people said your father should have been freed, that he didn't know what he was doing, that he was driven almost to insanity by the beating he had received and by the whiskey he had drunk.

Your mother was looking at you, and her voice was choking. She told you that you were born ahead of time. She told you that you were born the morning your father went up the river to prison. She said you were born in an ambulance between the Tombs and Bellevue. She said she wanted to commit suicide, that everything was all gone. She said she didn't want to go through life, and she didn't want you, her own son, to go through life, now that everyone was saying George Sands was a murderer. He wasn't a murderer. He wasn't a murderer, she sobbed. And the man reading the paper on the seat opposite looked up again.

Then your mother said other things. She asked you to please forgive her for not telling you about your father and everything else. She asked you to forgive her for putting you away when you were a baby because she couldn't help it. She told you she even changed her name to Anderson because she didn't want people talking. She wanted you to grow up and never hear about your father. She wanted you to be with nice people and never know that your father was in prison. That's why she had never told you she was your mother. She was going to tell you about it someday when your father got out of prison. But that was impossible now. Your father died about a month ago in prison. She knew then that it was time to be telling you the secret.

You looked at your mother now, and for the first time, all the knots began to unravel. You asked her about your father. You wanted to know how he died. What did he die of? So your mother told you. She said he just died of sickness. Then she said other things you wanted to remember all your life. She said that your father had a message for you about a month before he died. That was in April. This was the message. Your father wanted you to be a good man. He wanted you to grow up without hate or fear. He wanted you to remember him always because he had always loved you, though he had never seen you. He wanted you to forgive him for the mistakes he had made, and also he wanted you to remember that he bore no grudge against any man. And lastly, he wanted you to be proud that you were a Negro. That's the way God made you, and God needs no apologies. That's what your father said. That was all.

"And that's the whole story, George," Noella said.

Chubby faced his mother fully for the first time that afternoon and put his hand on her arm. He did not know how to put the words. He felt awkward. "It's all right. Everything's going to be all right for you, and Jean, and me."

Noella smiled then. It was the first time she had relaxed.

The Foundling

"I feel good, Georgie. For the first time in fourteen years I feel good."

The ferry was nearing New York.

Off to the west, the Statue of Liberty, caught in the flood of the afternoon sun, was poised against the sky. Chubby's eyes mirrored the tremendous figure that reared over the water lanes to the Atlantic. He wished the boat would draw closer. He would like to see the words he had memorized back at Mount Mary, the beautiful words he had recited in the play, the words that were inscribed on the Statue of Liberty. It was symbolic of America, that statue. It was a glorious triumphant figure fixed in sublime stance against the sky.

Liberty!

The cry was as loud as all the tongues of all the people, echoing out of the marshes, the plantations, off the hills, and down the mountains. It was a scream in the distant valley of the Nile and a shriek on the plains of Marathon. It was a shout on the fields of France and a groan in the basin of the Saar. It was a muttering in the ghettos, and a strangled sob that died in the throat of Nathan Hale as a hemp rope twisted out his life under our American stars.

Liberty!

It was not a provocative, demanding voice. It was not Anglo-Saxon or Nordic, Mongolian or Negroid. It was merely and essentially the voice of human hunger. And the hunger spoke of simple longings. It was saying: I want a place to live, a place to work, a place to be happy, a place to worship my God!

The Foundling

The world that afternoon was a ferry boat churning the waters of time. The world was a schooner chock full of Spaniards, Russians, French, Swedes, Germans, Chinese, Norwegians, Greeks, Irish, Poles. It was full of Whites and Browns, Blacks and Yellows. The boat-world was full of human beings. For these fleeting moments, it was a lovely afternoon boat-world. People were content. They were reading their newspapers. They were talking and laughing. They weren't thinking of putting Protestants to starboard and Catholics to portside, Jews forward and Negroes aft. It was the grandest five cent or five dollar excursion ride in the world on a stream that was running very close to a statue!

But one young Negro boy was wishing that the ferry would veer just a bit to the west. He wanted to read the words he had recited in a play. He wanted to tell his mother that he remembered every word. She would have been proud of him.

"You know what's written on the Statue of Liberty, mother?" Chubby asked.

"What, George?"

He recited it then. He said it with the self-conscious air of a boy who wanted to make his mother proud, now that they were formally acquainted. And these are the words Chubby Sands spoke:

"A mighty woman with a torch, whose flame
Is the imprisoned lightning, and her name
Mother of Exiles. From her beacon-hand
Glows world-wide welcome; her mild eyes command
The air-bridged harbor that twin cities frame.

The Foundling

'Keep, ancient lands, your storied pomp!' cries she
With silent lips. 'Give me your tired, your poor,
Your huddled masses yearning to breathe free,
The wretched refuse of your teeming shore.
Send these the homeless, tempest-tost to me.
I lift my lamp beside the golden door!' "

"Is that what it says on the statue, George?"

"Yes. That's what the Lady of Liberty says. But you got to get real close to the statue to see these words. The ferry never goes close enough."

PART 3

Chapter 14

"You're lost without Chub, aren't you, Peter?" Sister Crescentia asked a few weeks later.

"He was my best buddy, Sister."

"I know."

"He's working a paper route on Lenox Avenue, now, supporting his mother and sister."

"Sometimes I almost wish I could work that paper route with him."

The nun smiled easily. Then she asked a question that was like a thunderbolt.

"Would you like to spend the summer in Massachusetts, Peter?" Sister Crescentia hastened to add, "The Ross family would be glad to have you."

"The Ross family?"

"They're relatives of mine."

Massachusetts! The invitation was a complete surprise.

The Foundling

For a moment, Peter was tempted to tell her that his plans were already made. Jim Randall had promised to give him his favorite horse, Dan, again for the summer.

"Massachusetts, Sister?"

"Lynnford, Massachusetts. I'd like you to have the opportunity to enjoy a little family life. But it's up to you. Would you prefer to spend the summer here?"

Peter was touched by her concern for him. "I think I'd like to go, Sister."

"I'm sure you'll like Lynnford. They have a piano, too. You'll be able to keep up with your lessons. I'll give you the assignments."

The day came at last when Peter was to leave Mount Mary for the summer. The nuns, under the supervision of Sister Crescentia, heaped bags of figs, dates, peanuts, caramels, and Messengers of the Sacred Heart into a basket. He was proud of his valise. Sister Felicia confided that it was hers and that she was glad to let him take it. "And remember, that special flap is for your shirts," she advised. Sister Felicia was swell.

And Sister Crescentia was swell, too. She had weighed him down with manila envelopes bulging with gavottes, minuets, and selections from Bach.

"Don't lose that music," she warned. Then, offering him a small envelope, she said, "Here, Peter, don't buy too much candy with it."

"Thank you, Sister."

"And now," Sister Crescentia said, "we have a special surprise for you, Peter." She pressed the buzzer. The door

The Foundling

opened behind Peter, and Paul Taggart walked into the room.

"Mr. Taggart's going to take you all the way to Boston, Peter," Sister Crescentia announced.

"Mr. Taggart!" Peter shouted in joyous surprise.

Paul was laughing softly behind him.

"Mr. Taggart wants to take you in real style. You're going by boat."

Peter couldn't say a word. He was utterly filled with happiness.

The nuns waved to them when they sped out of the driveway in the station wagon. When Peter caught a glimpse of the north field at the gate, he was almost tempted to turn back. But Paul Taggart, his packed valise, the basket of fruit and candy, and the prospect of the boat trip mellowed the parting moment.

The big E of the Eastern Line was fluttering on the pennants at the North River pier. Walking up the gangplank of the S. S. *New York* behind Mr. Taggart, Peter stepped into a brilliant new world of lounging rooms, thick carpets and important looking gentlemen in nautical jackets. Now, he felt, he was truly launched on the broad seas of life.

Mr. Taggart laughed when he jumped at the warning blast of the boat whistle. It was the loudest sound Peter had ever heard, and he secretly envied a boy next to him who kept chewing gum without losing a beat.

Sitting in the dining room that evening, Mr. Taggart was in high spirits. "This is our first dinner on water, Peter, so let's make it a good one."

The Foundling

The boy who had been chewing gum that afternoon was sitting at the next table. From the speed with which he delivered his order, Peter judged he had long been acquainted with the mystery of menus.

After due consideration, Peter ordered, among other things, six cherrystone clams. He wasn't too sure what cherrystone clams were, but they sounded all right and besides they must be the proper thing to eat, since he had overheard the boy at the next table order them, too.

When the waiter had left, Mr. Taggart began to trace the ship's route for him over the table linen. The salt and pepper shakers were respectively Throgg's Neck and Sand's Point. After sailing around the pepper, they proceeded eastward between Mr. Taggart's knife and Peter's clam fork. Mr. Taggart's knife was New York, Connecticut, Rhode Island and Massachusetts all in one piece; the clam fork to the south was Long Island with Montauk Point jutting out into the Atlantic on the lower prong. The bottle of horseradish was Martha's Vineyard and Nantucket Island was a toothpick lying to the southeast.

"But don't mind Nantucket, Peter. We don't go near it. Instead, we shoot up here into Buzzard's Bay and then . . ." Mr. Taggart placed a lane of matches across the napkin and, running his fingers over them, he continued, "And then we go through Cape Cod Canal."

Cape Cod Canal was indeed a marvel, since Paul impressed upon him how much of the napkin they would have been required to sail around if there were no canal. Several points of interest were then indicated—New London, New-

The Foundling

port, and the approximate location of Plymouth Rock. From the matchsticks, it was then a comparatively short sail to the ketchup, which proved to be Boston.

By that time, the waiter returned. After he made a quick private grace before meals, Peter opened his eyes for the first time in his life upon clams on the half shell. He stared at the horrible, spineless, shapeless things for fully ten seconds. They were neatly packed in ice, but Peter was sure that no amount of refrigeration could ever undo whatever had already happened to them.

"Are these cherrystone clams?" he finally asked Mr. Taggart.

"Yes, I'm sure they're cherrystones, Peter," he said. Then he lifted a clam with the fork and showed Peter the dark cherry tint of the shell, but even this identification did nothing to dispel Peter's conviction that there was something dreadfully wrong somewhere.

"Do they look fresh to you, Mr. Taggart?" he asked, affecting a gourmet's nonchalance.

Paul inspected the clams critically. "About as fresh as you could expect, Peter."

Perhaps that was the trouble. They looked too utterly fresh. He glanced around uneasily at the boy at the next table. He was already on his fifth clam, and what was worse, he seemed actually to be relishing them.

"One good way to tell if they're really fresh is to squirt a little lemon juice on them," Paul suggested.

Peter squeezed the lemon.

"There you are! Did you see it move, Peter?"

The Foundling

Move!

"Lemon juice will do that to a clam freshly opened," Paul explained.

"Do you mean these clams are *alive?*"

"Yes, Peter."

That was more than enough for Peter. His eyes betrayed him, and Mr. Taggart began to laugh. "Didn't you ever eat clams before, Peter?"

"No. I never even saw them before," he confessed. "Maybe you'd better eat them, Mr. Taggart," he suggested guardedly, lest the brave boy who had now finished his might overhear.

A few minutes later, Peter settled for soup beneath the amused glance of the waiter.

After they had listened to the orchestra and watched the dancers for a while, Mr. Taggart chose two chairs beneath the Captain's cabin and they sat with their jackets pulled about their necks against the strong breeze. Below them a sailor was keeping vigil on the deck and once, when he signalled the bridge, a bright beam of light cut into the darkness and searched the waters. Sure enough, the sailor had seen something. A log was floating on the waves, and a sea gull was standing on it. The light was held on the log for a few moments and then it blinked out and the ship steamed on in the night. How reassuring, Peter mused, to think that you could go to sleep knowing that the unwearying eyes of men were keeping watch over the waves.

Finally, Paul Taggart spoke. "Peter, I was thinking about something you said one day last year."

The Foundling

Peter turned in his chair and faced Mr. Taggart.

He was having difficulty lighting a cigarette with his one hand, and Peter shielded the flame of the match for him in the cup of his fingers. The light from the stateroom fell along the side of Paul's face and Peter saw that he was smiling. "From now on, call me Paul. Do you mind, Peter?"

"No." But he still wondered what Paul meant. "What did I say?"

"One day back at the Mount I asked you if anyone ever wanted to adopt you. Do you remember the day?"

"Yes."

"You told me you didn't want to leave Mount Mary because you wanted me to adopt you."

"That's right, Paul. I did want you to adopt me."

Mr. Taggart inhaled deeply and his eyes wandered out over the dark water. "Did you ever think for a moment, Peter, that I didn't want to have you? To have you for my own son?"

"No," Peter said weakly. "But you just never asked and that's why I kept waiting."

"Do you know why I never asked?"

"No, I don't."

"I'm not a Catholic, Peter."

"You're not a Catholic, Mr. Taggart—Paul?"

"No, I'm not a Catholic." He puffed the cigarette slowly. "Didn't they ever tell you that at the Mount?"

"No."

They said nothing further for a few minutes, and Peter was thoroughly uncomfortable.

The Foundling

Finally, Mr. Taggart spoke. "That's why I never adopted you. That's why I couldn't adopt you."

So that's how it was. All those years during which he had waited for Paul to ask him to go home with him and Ellen were explained now in that one sentence. It was simple, now. Protestants just couldn't adopt Catholics and Catholics are not allowed to adopt Protestants.

The night sky was wide and brilliant with stars, and far ahead the shore signals were blinking at regular intervals. Shortly before it was time to go to bed, Paul broke the silence.

"Peter, I don't know what plans you have for the future, but whatever they are, I want you to know that you can always count on me to help."

It was said so sincerely and simply that Peter did not know how to answer.

"I know now that you love music and Sister Crescentia has confided to me that you have been gifted with great talent in it," Paul continued. "And if that's what you want most in life, I'll see to it that you get the best training that money can buy."

Peter tried to thank him, but Paul's strong left hand reached out and closed over his fingers. "Here, take this," he said. "Maybe I won't have time to give it to you in the morning."

It was a small package.

Peter opened it. Under the faint light from the stateroom a golden gleam caught his eye. "A wrist watch!"

"Ellen was the one who picked it out."

The Foundling

"Thanks, Paul," Peter said, realizing how futile a word it was.

"That's all right, Peter," Paul brushed aside the boy's gratitude. "Just wind it regularly. It'll keep good time."

Two hours later, Paul Taggart was asleep in the bunk over Peter's head. There were many faint and friendly sounds for the boy that night; the creaking of the cabin, the singing swish of water running to white foam in the darkness, the lulling hum of the great engines that sped the S.S. *New York* to Boston. But by far the friendliest of all the sounds was the regular breathing of a man whom among all the men of the earth, Peter wanted most for a father.

"Good night, Paul," he whispered; and then he fell asleep with the wrist watch ticking against his ear.

Chapter 15

SUMMER ENDS all too quickly in New England. That last night, Peter sat by a window in the house at Lynnford trying to compose a letter. A fitful wind with rain in it was blowing from the northeast and though it was too dark to see him, he knew that O. G. Healy was having a tough time of it on the roof. O. G. Healy was the weather-vane man. He was one foot high and he was forever sitting in his lumber wagon with his solid oak horses poised to run to all parts of the compass.

Peter wrote the first draft of the letter in pencil. Tomorrow, he would copy it in ink and give it to Mrs. Ross in a sealed envelope. He would address it: To Mr. and Mrs. Ross.

"Dear Mr. and Mrs. Ross,
"I want to thank you very much for your kindness to me. When I came here three months ago, you made

me feel right at home. Even that first night in the kitchen, Mrs. Ross, when you took the cinder out of my eye, you made me feel at home, because you said the other kids sometimes got cinders in their eyes also, and I wanted to be like them as much as I could.

"I want to thank Eddie, Jack, Mark and Barbara for their kindness to me also.

"When I go back to Mount Mary I will have many things to tell Sister Crescentia. I will tell her that you were asking for her, and I will tell her about all the swell times we had together, especially about the swell times we had in the auto.

"There is only one thing I hope you won't say to Sister Crescentia, and that is about Mr. Mowgler's grocery store, because . . ."

Helen Spalding was the reason for this request. He did not know that she was Helen Spalding at first. She walked into church that Sunday morning like a breath of primrose and when she knelt in the pew beside him with her wide straw hat bobbing a brim of daisies at him, Peter completely forgot it was the Fifth Sunday after Pentecost. When the collection basket came around, he decided to put a dime instead of a nickel in it, since a dime made a more expensive clink, and there was no harm in giving a girl a good impression. He also rustled the pages of his missal quite loudly at the Preface, not only because the priest was a good bit ahead of him, and he had to catch up, but also because there was a beautiful picture that came just before the Canon, and this would undoubtedly inspire Helen to follow the Mass with a missal as he was doing, and not with a rosary as she was doing.

The Foundling

After Mass was over, Peter wanted to ask Eddie Ross if he knew the young lady who had knelt beside him, but, fearing that Eddie might suspect he was too interested in her, he asked Barbara instead.

He said, in an off-hand way, "Boy, the hats some people wear in church!"

Barbara looked at him quizzically.

"Like for instance the girl who knelt beside me. Did you see the awful hat she was wearing, Barbara?"

Barbara frowned. "Oh, she always wears those flappy things."

"Nothing but daisies all over it, huh, Barbara?"

"Aren't they awful, Peter?"

Barbara was irritatingly enigmatic about the identity of the lovely princess. Throwing diplomacy to the winds, Peter asked, "Just who is she anyway?"

"Helen Spalding."

Helen Spalding. What a musical, magical name. Helen Spalding.

He fell asleep that night in the friendly home in Lynnford with O. G. Healy spinning and squeaking on a romantic southerly wind.

The following day, Peter discovered where Helen lived. It was a little brown house with roses set in lattices on both sides of the road entrance. He walked by it at least a dozen times that afternoon, hoping she might come out on the lawn to knit or read a book or anything. Helen, however, did not appear.

It was in this perplexing situation that the idea of saddling

The Foundling

and riding Samson struck Peter as the proper romantic approach to a maiden's heart. Samson was a big, black horse that had gained a bad reputation for running away and also for kicking. He belonged to Mr. Bodiou, the French farmer who lived at the outskirts of Lynnford. On the following Sunday (the Sunday Peter missed Helen in church), when Mr. Bodiou and his family were far over the New England hills in their automobile, Peter took the liberty of borrowing the horse from the pasture.

It was to be a perfectly planned ceremony. Since Helen had lived in Massachusetts all her life, Peter was certain that the Paul Revere touch would warm her beautiful heart. There would be, first, the terrific pounding of Samson's shoes as they charged down the road. About twenty yards past her house, he would rein in the magnificent steed, and turn him back. There would be another terrific gallop, and Helen would come running out on the lawn exclaiming, "It's Samson! That boy who is staying with Mr. and Mrs. Ross is actually riding Samson!"

That afternoon, however, Samson had other ideas. He went charging past Helen's house according to schedule, but when Peter tried to stop him, Samson kept right on running. As a matter of fact, Samson did not stop running until he had thundered up an embankment and leaped over a stone wall, a quarter of a mile away from Helen's house. After stumbling momentarily, the horse came to a halt.

Samson limped all the way back much to Peter's disgrace. It was only after he slipped the bridle off the horse in the Bodiou pasture, that Peter saw blood running in a stream over the right hind hoof. The horse had wounded himself against the stone wall.

When Peter crawled into bed that night, the awful picture of the crippled animal sent fright through him. Samson was Bodiou's only work horse, and he was the culprit who had maimed him.

Samson was limping the next morning, and after the veterinarian attended him on Tuesday, a visit which cost Mr. Bodiou two dollars, the horse was still crippled.

That night, Peter began to measure the enormity of his crime. Since Samson was declared to be unfit for work for many days by the veterinarian, Mr. Bodiou had been obliged to borrow a horse from the neighboring farm. This meant more expense for the poor farmer, and realizing he was already responsible for the veterinarian's account, Peter reached a nadir of despair as he tried to calculate the staggering cost of that Sunday gallop.

All this harrowing business, however, did not lessen his devotion for Helen Spalding. At night, while O. G. Healy squeaked on the breeze, he dreamed of her. Having failed to attract her attention with Samson (she had actually been in Framingham that afternoon), his only hopes lay in seeing her again next Sunday at Mass. His greatest dread was that she might be already engaged to some millionaire's son with white slacks and white shoes. In that case, with only Sunday mornings to count on, the business of capturing her heart would be even more difficult. But this was life, he philosophized. It was a hard battle. Indeed, it was only fitting, he reasoned, that a girl so beautiful as Helen should not be won easily. Samson had already contributed more than his share of difficulties and Peter shuddered to think how many more were probably around the corner.

On a piece of paper, Peter figured the methods by which he could make restitution for Samson's crippled leg. The expenses Mr. Bodiou would be obliged to meet in paying the veterinarian, in feeding Samson and in hiring another horse, were added in one column. It was a lot of money. If Peter sold newspapers for the rest of the summer, he would not even come close to paying for the damages. Selling newspapers was patently out of the question.

Mr. Mowgler's grocery store leaped suddenly into his mind. Working for Mr. Mowgler might be a more profitable business.

To think was to act. "Hello, Mr. Mowgler," Peter said, the following morning.

"Hello."

"Do you need a boy to help you?"

"No."

Peter was walking out of the store when Mr. Mowgler called him back.

"Who are you?" he asked.

"Peter Lane. I'm staying with Mr. and Mrs. Ross."

"Did they send you here?"

"No, sir."

The man pinched his fat cheeks and seemed to be pondering a question. "Have you had any experience?"

"Just a little bit, Mr. Mowgler. But I can be a good grocery store man and fix your window like they fix them in New

York." Peter was referring to pyramids of canned peaches which he had seen on display. "And I can learn the places where you keep the different groceries real fast and the names of the customers."

A slow grin spread across Mr. Mowgler's face. "How much would you work for if I gave you a job?"

"Oh, six dollars a week." He wondered if he had gone too high.

"All right. Six dollars a week. Tomorrow, you come here at seven o'clock."

Mr. and Mrs. Ross were surprised when Peter announced that night that he had decided to work at Mowgler's for the rest of the summer.

"But, Peter, we wanted you to have a vacation," Mrs. Ross said.

"Oh, that's all right. I like to work, Mrs. Ross," he answered. Her blue eyes were studying him inquiringly, but he resisted the temptation to tell her the whole story.

He went to bed that night, half troubled that he had made a decision without consulting her, and half glad that he was started on the long road of restitution which would pay for the injured leg of a horse, and which might possibly win the heart of a beautiful girl. Before he went to sleep, he remembered remorsefully that he had not practised his piano lessons, and Sister Crescentia began to brood admonishingly in the quiet of the room.

O. G. Healy was quiet on the roof that night; there was no wind abroad.

The Foundling

A few mornings later there was intoxicating news. Peter was standing behind Mr. Mowgler's counter with a pencil over his ear and an apron tied according to the smartest grocery store traditions. Mr. Mowgler was thumbing a small book.

"Mrs. Drury wants half a peck of potatoes, five pounds of sugar, and a pound of butter."

"Yes, Mr. Mowgler," Peter said, making the notations.

"And Mrs. Spalding . . ."

Mrs. Spalding!

". . . wants a bag of flour, a pound of lard, a pound of coffee, two jars of grape jelly and a dozen lemons."

"Yes, Mr. Mowgler."

It was a joyous surprise to hear that Mrs. Spalding patronized Mr. Mowgler's store, and Peter was hoping against hope that, when he delivered the order, Helen herself would come to the door. He fondled the Spalding lemons, dusted the Spalding jelly jars, put an extra piece of wax paper about the Spalding lard, and bravely set forth.

Fifteen-year-old Barbara Ross, who insisted upon accompanying him on several of his grocery deliveries, proved to be particularly annoying that morning. She had a habit of riding her bike zig-zag fashion along the road, carrying on a running conversation that was most unbusinesslike. When Peter saw the familiar braids flying in the distance that morning, his heart sank.

"Hello," Barbara said, cutting a close circle around his grocery cart with her bike.

"Hello," he answered coolly.

The Foundling

"Want any help?"

"No."

"Where you going?"

"Straight ahead," Peter answered, hoping she would take the hint. Helen Spalding might even want to talk with him privately. The dismal possibility of having Barbara spoil it all by calling him "Noodles," which she sometimes did, was anything but a pleasing prospect.

"My brother Eddie is playing first base at Partridge's field this morning," she announced, making another circle around his cart.

Eddie could be playing first, second, and third for all Peter cared.

"And you know where we're going next Sunday?"

Sunday didn't matter now that Helen's house was in view.

"We're going to Plymouth."

Plymouth was not half so attractive as the roses which were still twining about the lattices at Helen's doorway.

"I asked my father to take you and me to Plymouth, Peter."

Helen Spalding wasn't visible at any of the windows, and Peter had a fearful suspicion that she might have gone to Framingham again.

"Would you like to go to Plymouth, Peter?" Barbara asked from the other side of the road.

But Peter was too busy combing his hair to answer her question.

Barbara brought the bicycle to a stop. She must have read Peter's mind because she looked curiously at the Spalding house for an instant. Turning her dark eyes on him, she said, "I could have brought you some vaseline for your hair, Peter. Helen likes it that way."

Before he could remind her that delivery boys had to be neat and presentable at all times, Barbara drove off with her dark braids flying pertly in the breeze.

Peter's breath was coming fast when he pushed the Spalding bell. Would she or wouldn't she open the door? From far back in the house he heard the footsteps approaching. They were light and rhythmic. Surely they must be Helen's footsteps.

Slowly the door opened, and . . . it was she. Helen. A vision of loveliness in blue gingham.

"Groceries for Mrs. Spalding," Peter said, reverently.

"Yes, I'll take them," she answered.

Peter almost tripped over the threshold when he placed the package in her hands.

"Thank you," she said, and her blue eyes beamed deep into his. Then she was gone.

Peter whistled happily all the way back to Mowgler's. How willingly would he have spent hours dusting jelly jars and polishing lemons just for one smile from Helen.

"O, and we'll have a Nuptial Mass, and we'll kneel on the plush kneelers, and the organ will be playing *Here Comes the Bride* for us, and Father Duane will sprinkle holy water on the ring that I will buy for you if I ever get Samson's leg paid off."

O. G. Healy was jockeying his horses on a gentle breeze

The Foundling

that evening when Peter came home from work. A few minutes later, he discovered Mrs. Ross pulling down the sheets in his room as she always did.

"Hello, Mrs. Ross."

"Hello, Peter." Her voice was cheerful. "Did you have a hard day?"

"Not so hard."

Then a sly note of amusement colored her words. "You certainly believe in being well prepared, don't you, Peter?"

He did not understand.

She pointed to the dresser on which there were three combs, a jar of vaseline, and a bottle of Tame Tiger hair oil.

Peter was dumbfounded for a moment. "Where did they come from?"

"Didn't you put them there?"

"No, Mrs. Ross."

It was then that he remembered the peculiar smirk Barbara had given him on the stairs.

When he sat opposite her at supper that night, her dark eyes were searching his face for his reaction. "Will you have some butter, Barbara?" he asked, pretending to be completely oblivious to her prank. The maneuver worked. It was evident that his complacency annoyed her.

"No, thanks," she answered almost sharply, and the entire Ross family looked at her.

"Women are peculiar creatures," Peter confided to O. G. Healy that night, and the little lumber man squeaked an unmistakable affirmative.

As the days went by in Lynnford, the very texture of

The Foundling

Peter's life seemed to be interwoven with the precious personality of Helen Spalding. Mowgler's grocery store was a veritable shrine wherein her presence spoke to him from banked choirs of Fig Newtons and cans of corn and tomatoes. He never looked at a jar of grape jelly without recalling the depth of her eyes; and the lard was a sacroscanct substance, soft and immaculate and full of that first memory wherein her voice said "Thank you" over the threshold of her home.

Then came the historic day. Helen Spalding herself walked into the store just at the time when Mr. Mowgler, happily, was at lunch. She had a Boston terrier at the end of a leash, and the dog's barking frightened Mr. Mowgler's cat.

"Quiet, Bobby," Helen admonished in most persuasive tones.

"That's all right," Peter said, perfectly willing to have a thousand cats scared by Helen's dog.

Helen paused over the candy counter. "Do you have jelly beans?" she asked.

Jelly beans. Why, if Mr. Mowgler were out of jelly beans, Peter would have run all the way to Framingham for them. He would have run even to Worcester. But they had jelly beans.

"Yes, Miss Spalding. We have jelly beans."

"I'll have a nickel's worth, please."

"Yes, Miss Spalding."

The small candy shovel which Mr. Mowgler had taught him to use with precise avoirdupois discretion (since "it is

The Foundling

the depression and we can't be Santa Claus,") seemed monstrously inadequate to express the length, depth, and height of his love for Helen.

"A nickel's worth?" Peter asked.

"Yes."

Peter dug into the jelly beans and came up with a brimming shovel. Then pouring them into a bag, he paused dramatically, so that she might appreciate the extremes to which devotion was leading him.

"That's a nickel's worth," he said, weighing the bag professionally in his hand. Then with a debonair shrug at the capitalistic system of business for profit, he scooped another full shovel of jelly beans and flung them into the bag.

"How much?" she asked in tones of wonderment. It was apparent she had recognized his generosity.

"How much?" he repeated. It was then that he summoned all the tender nuances of affection, liberality, magnanimity and benevolence into his voice. "Nothing," he said.

"Nothing?" she asked.

"Nothing, Miss Spalding. Those jelly beans are on me."

"You're very kind," she remarked smilingly. When she walked out of the store, her dog Bobby was barking as sweetly as it is possible for a Boston terrier to bark.

The matter of straightening out his conscience was a minor one for Peter. When Benjamin Franklin said "a penny saved is a penny earned," he must have had Mr. Mowgler's grocery store in mind, and because the grocer was committed irrevocably to this policy and had it printed on a card in the store window, and because, also, it was a sin to be too free with another man's jelly beans, Peter promptly put ten cents of his own into the cash register.

"I hope she'll come back for some more jelly beans," he prayed that night.

Mount Mary, Sister Crescentia, and the many limitations of institutional life rose up threateningly into his thoughts that summer night in Lynnford. The fragrance of the orchards, freighted with the small Baldwins, Sour Porters, and Red Astrichans was in the air. Helen would still be here when the frost was helping to make the apples ripe. She would be walking over the snow with a wool scarf about her neck and her face would be even more beautiful in the winter. Peter envied the orchards, the hedges, and the Lynnford countryside. He envied the people of Lynnford and Mr. Mowgler in particular. They would always be close to Helen Spalding. "Maybe she won't remember that I gave her a dime's worth of jelly beans for nothing," he thought. "Maybe, when I go back to Mount Mary, she'll go off and marry some son of a millionaire with white slacks and white shoes."

O. G. Healy, his inseparable weather-vane companion, was no help that night. "Maybe," he squeaked shrilly in the shifting breeze. "Maybe."

Chapter 16

THE DAYS passed that summer, sometimes bright with promise, sometimes dark with doubt.

Then came the memorable Sunday evening in late August, three days before Peter's departure from Lynnford. Many devious and painstaking plans had been made for that evening, he was to discover later. They went back to the night when Peter was rubbing oil into Jackie's first baseman's glove. Mr. Ross was dozing in his favorite chair by the window, and Mrs. Ross was writing a letter. Barbara, sitting at the table with a magazine in her hands, looked across the room from time to time. The quiet, restful New England Sunday evening was broken only by the cozy conversation the boys were having in the corner.

"Do you know anything about baseball, Peter?" Jackie asked.

"I sure do, Jackie," Peter answered, smoothing the oil

into the pocket of the glove. The youngster listened intently while Peter told him about the catches Bill Terry used to make in the Polo Grounds when Freddy Lindstrom threw some fast ones into the dirt. But Jackie wanted to hear about the Braves and Red Sox.

Barbara walked across the room at that moment. "See this?" she began pointing to a dress pattern in the magazine she was holding.

"What about it?" Peter asked.

"Do you like it?"

"The dress you mean?"

"Yes."

"It's all right, Barbara." The answer could not be called enthusiastic.

Barbara walked back to her chair.

Jackie was eager to hear more about baseball players, so Peter told him of other great champions he had seen when the Saint Vincent de Paul men took the older boys at Mount Mary to the games. "Did you ever hear of Travis Jackson, Jackie?"

"No."

"Well, Jackson could throw a ball from short to first faster than *that*," he snapped his fingers to indicate the lightning interval, "and he could hit, too."

"Yeah?" Jackie asked, admiration lighting his small face.

"Yeah."

Barbara again interrupted the discussion. "How do you like that one, Peter?" she asked, pointing to another pattern.

"That's a nice dress, Barbara."

"You really think it's pretty?"

Peter wanted to tell Jackie about the day Babe Ruth had given him his autograph at the Yankee Stadium. "It's about the prettiest dress I've ever seen," he said heartily, hoping Barbara would go away. Her dark eyes scrutinized him for a second and then, smiling easily, she walked quickly out of the room.

The preparations for that memorable Sunday night in late August started as early as that.

Barbara began innocently enough by asking a normal question one morning. "Are you going out with Mark and Eddie tonight?"

"No, Barbara. I've some piano lessons to practise."

"Then you'll be home all evening."

"Yes."

That night Peter was sitting alone before the piano running through some exercises, when Barbara entered the room. He was engrossed in trying to make a transposition and he was fast approaching that stage where he imagined himself in Aeolian Hall rendering Schumann's entire *Fantasy in C Major* with his left hand alone, a feat which would not only have startled the entire music world, but which would also have revolutionized the very principles of physics which prohibit one thumb from playing C and G at exactly the same time.

Barbara coughed behind him to attract attention.

He spun slowly on the piano stool. "Did you say something, Barbara?"

The Foundling

"No," she answered.

He turned back to his music, and she coughed again; it was a most insistent kind of cough. Finally, she said, "How do you like my new dress?"

Peter gave it a brief inspection. "It's nice, Barbara," he said. "Oh, by the way, did you see that *Moonlight Sonata* music I left here last night?"

Her eyes were suddenly glinting furiously. "No, I didn't see your old *Moonlight Sonata* music." She walked out of the room quickly, and when Peter heard her door slam over his head, he shrugged and dismissed her simply as an odd and moody creature.

About twenty minutes later, she returned wearing a different dress. "You like music, don't you?" she asked, her face unusually calm.

"Yes, Barbara. I'm going to spend all my life at it if I can."

After a few minutes' pause, she said, "Mother says you can play the piano real well."

Peter was surprised at this bit of relayed praise.

"Would you mind if I invited some friends to hear you play?" Barbara asked.

"Friends?"

"Close friends."

The suggestion was frightening. Though he had frequently dreamed of being only too willing to appear for the tenth encore before applauding thousands, the prospect of actually playing before a Lynnford audience suddenly scared him stiff.

The Foundling

"I'm sure you would enjoy playing something for Genevieve Sheehan and Helen Spalding and Margaret . . ."

"Did you say Helen Spalding?"

"Yes."

"You mean . . . Helen Spalding will come *here* in *this house* and listen to . . ."

Barbara was visibly annoyed. "What's so different about her? She comes here and drinks our ginger ale and eats our Boston Brownies, just like anyone else."

This surely was an answer to prayer. Helen Spalding. Sitting there in that very chair. Looking at him and listening to his . . .

"Would you like me to ask them?" Barbara repeated.

"Well, sure! Of course, Barbara," Peter declared, beaming with pleasure.

The preparations for that Sunday evening in late August were feverish and multiple. Mrs. Ross, at Barbara's suggestion, prepared a bowl of punch (six quarts of ginger ale, two bottles of grape juice, and four lemons), as well as a giant, triple-layer, ribbon cake with music notes in frosted vanilla to mark the occasion fittingly.

About a half hour before the arrival of the guests, Mark Ross, Barbara's oldest brother, called Peter aside. He prefaced his remarks with an admission that he was not "exactly an authority on music" but said that he felt that the selections Peter intended to play might be a bit "highbrow."

"Highbrow, Mark? What do you mean?"

"You know, sort of heavy," he said.

"Heavy?" Peter was puzzled.

The Foundling

"If you could sort of mix it up a bit, Peter . . ."

"You see," Mark sat back in the chair and dropped his voice to a confiding level, "you see, Peter, you have to understand that most people like their music lighter." But Peter's motive with his music was to please Sister Crescentia and Helen Spalding.

The guests arrived in buzzing groups and were seated in the parlor. When Peter entered Mr. and Mrs. Austin, the next-door neighbors, Mr. and Mrs. Mowgler, and a dozen young ladies were occupying chairs in a tight semi-circle about the piano.

Mr. Austin beamed across the room. "I heard you, Peter," he said. "I heard you playing my old friend Bach, night after night."

Mr. Austin's short remark was a consolation that leaped out of that small sea of faces, and it left Peter immeasurably sure of himself.

Barbara was leaning against the wall beneath the large picture of Uncle Mark Ross. Her face was paler than usual, and Peter knew she was watching him.

"Hello, Barbara," he began, trying to ease the tension that was slowly mounting with each passing minute.

Helen Spalding arrived, accompanied by Mrs. Spalding, a gracious lady with silver hair and a voice that carried melodiously across the hum of the company. A brief interchange of greetings followed. Helen sat next to Barbara and smiled in Peter's direction.

Then Peter sat at the piano.

A pause.

The Foundling

He began, and a shocking, disastrous instant followed. It might have been his fingers; it might have been nervousness. It might have been a dozen indefinable tricks of a recalcitrant fourth finger. But it was none of these. It was the piano instead. It rang with a discordant clang.

"What's the trouble, Peter?" Mr. Ross asked.

"I think there's something wrong with the piano, sir." Again he struck the keys and again the same mixture of muted pots and pans broke over the room. "The piano is all choked up, Mr. Ross," Peter said and hurried out of the parlor in confusion and, he felt, disgrace.

Five minutes later, Mr. Ross consoled him in his room. "It's nothing to worry about, Peter. The piano is an old one anyway."

"I don't understand what happened to that piano, Mr. Ross. It was all right this evening."

"Probably dried up and snapped apart. I'll have Joe Dunnigan look at it in the morning."

Joe Dunnigan? Who was Joe Dunnigan? Joe Dunnigan could not have healed this mortal wound. Not even Bach himself, if he had come rushing into the parlor with a Steinway, could have undone the disaster which had fallen so heavily on all Peter's musical dreams.

"They understand, Peter," Mr. Ross said. "It wasn't your fault. And we're giving them plenty of punch and cake, so they're enjoying it anyway."

Punch and cake! Helen Spalding didn't want punch and cake. Helen wanted to hear him play.

"Come on down stairs, Peter," Mr. Ross said.

"No, thanks, Mr. Ross. I think I'd better . . ." But he couldn't finish it. At fifteen years of age, he did it again. Peter cried. It was pride, and it was a bit of weakness, too, which is not quite on the verge of being pride. Only one who knows the very narrow channels of the young mind, like Father Duane, could understand how Peter felt.

O. G. Healy was lost that night in the loud laughing of the people beneath Peter's room. Mrs. Ross knocked at the door shortly afterwards, but Peter pretended to be asleep. He was wondering how Helen was enjoying the punch and cake. "She must know that it was not my fault," he mused. "I hope she will come into Mowgler's soon and I can explain that the piano was worse than an ash can."

But he knew, somehow, she would never come into Mowgler's. So he fell asleep with a wish that he was back at Mount Mary with his horse, Dan, Sister Crescentia and Sister Felicia, and Jim Randall.

Two days later, he walked out to Mr. Bodiou's farm. The sun was sinking in a bright orange glow. It was the day before he was to leave Lynnford, and the world seemed beautiful and sad as he walked over the roads he had come to know so well.

The money he had earned at Mowgler's, twenty-eight dollars, was wrapped in an envelope. There was also a note to Mr. Bodiou. Peter had learned that Samson's injury had cost much less than what he fearfully estimated after the accident. Since he did not want the Ross family to know what he was up to, he hurried out of the house when no one was looking. It was better, anyway, to walk to Bodiou's farm alone because it was a soft, colorful evening, designed for a lone road, and a walking stick in your hand, and a half a dozen special thoughts in your head.

The old sadness was coming back to Peter again as he trudged by the cottages of Lynnford that evening. And when the road ran out of the town to the wider spaces where the whole of the west was spread with the splendor of evening, he had a passionate hunger to walk forever and ever. He loved the west. He never looked into the immensity of those flaming skies without dreaming of the houses, out there, set in the green curves of the hills. And they must be beautiful pasture fences, running in straight lines of cedar to the ultimate knolls on the horizon.

Theresa Bordano, with her blind eyes catching the glow of a music lamp she could not see, seemed to be playing the organ again. It was an organ, rich and vibrant, and it was reaching out gently with its wide arms to the land. It was cool music, cool as the tall shadows of the pines; it was as warm as the face of someone he loved smiling through a window at him.

"Maybe, I'll never be happy," Peter thought. "Maybe, I'll walk and walk, looking for the place where the sunset ends, and I'll never find it. Maybe, if I walked clear around the world, I'd come right back here to Lynnford and . . . Helen."

Yes, that is what he would do. He would come back to Lynnford again. He would come back, perhaps, in some winter time when the snow was spread thickly over the

The Foundling

earth. It would be in the chill, gray glare of dusk when houses begin to wink their cheery lights at the roads, and when smoke comes curling out of all the chimneys in the towns. He would come when life in New England was gathered at the firesides; when the sounds were the small, happy sounds of chestnuts crackling on the hearths and tea kettles singing on the stoves. He would come into the house with the cold breath of the wind about him, grown to manhood and strength. And he would find her, Helen, and he would speak to her, no longer afraid to make a man's profession of love. For love, according to Father Duane, was a good thing. Love was something that made God a baby in the arms of Mary. Love made families, and firesides, and houses that blinked with cheery warmth from millions and millions of windows. Love was good.

Thus did Peter dream that evening on the way to Bodiou's farm.

He was startled to hear a voice behind him when he leaned against the field fence overlooking Mr. Bodiou's pasture. It was Barbara Ross.

"Hello," she said.

"Hello," Peter answered, trying to conceal his surprise.

"I followed you, Peter."

It was evident she had followed him, and Peter found himself wondering what excuse he could give for coming this distance. He did not want her to suspect anything about the Samson debacle.

She leaned against the fence and looked out over the field. "Are you mad at me for following you?"

The Foundling

"No."

"Really?"

"I'm not mad at you, Barbara. Why should I be mad?"

Barbara frowned and continued to look over the field. "You're going away tomorrow, Peter."

"I know."

"I wanted to tell you something before you left."

"Is that why you followed me?"

"Yes." She turned her dark eyes to him, and he looked away. "You're going to be mad when I tell you, Peter."

His curiosity was aroused. "No, I won't."

"Yes, you will."

There was another long silence, and then he saw she was crying.

"What's the matter with you, Barbara?"

"I'm no good," she choked. "I'm no good, because I've committed a sin."

"Sin?"

"Yes." She sniffled some more. "It's on account of you."

"Me!"

"Yes." Barbara leaned on the fence with her eyes buried in her handkerchief. "I spoiled last Sunday night for you."

"What do you mean?"

"The piano." She was wailing sincerely now. "The piano. I put spoons and forks inside the piano. I didn't want you to play for Helen Spalding."

"So *that's* what was wrong with the piano?"

"Yes."

The Foundling

There was a long silence punctuated by more sniffles and sobs. "I couldn't help it, Peter. I wanted you to . . . to . . ."

But she never finished the sentence. Instead, she turned away and cried even more loudly.

"What's the matter with you, Barbara?"

She would not answer.

"Stop crying like that. If people see you, they'll blame me."

This brought a fresh outburst, and Peter decided that under the circumstances, there was nothing to do but look out over the fields and say nothing.

For fully three minutes, they waited there.

"You better go home, Barbara," he suggested finally.

Without saying a word, she walked quietly over the road.

Two hours later, long after he had delivered the envelope to the puzzled wife of Mr. Bodiou, Peter sat in his room with a pencil in his hand. O. G. Healey was still spinning on his roost in the night, and Peter was finishing the letter which tomorrow he would copy in ink and give to Mrs. Ross in a sealed envelope.

"There is only one thing I hope you won't say to Sister Crescentia, and that is about Mr. Mowgler's grocery store, because I had a special reason for working there and someday I will tell you what I did with the money I saved.

"Thanks again, Mr. and Mrs. Ross, for your kindness to me, and I am sure I will come back and see you again some day, because I like Lynnford, and I think everybody in New England is nice. Some day when I am able, I will pay you back for everything you have done for me. I will buy Mr. Ross a pipe, and Mrs. Ross a coat, and Jackie a bike, and Eddie a watch fob, and Mark a

The Foundling

ukulele. And for Barbara I'll maybe buy a whole set of forks and spoons, sterling silver and guaranteed not to rust. Good-bye.

"Yours sincerely
"Peter Lane"

Chapter 17

It was a November night in 1933.

Chubby's secret dream was outlined neatly on page seven of the magazine. He had already saved seven dollars and a quarter toward making the dream come true. Right now, however, he was watching his mother put on her coat. He hid the magazine beneath the algebra book before he spoke.

"Mom, I invited Peter Lane to have dinner with us, day after tomorrow."

Noella faced him quickly. "Why did you do that?"

"Because I haven't seen him for six months, and Thanksgiving day is . . ."

"George, you got no sense."

The boy frowned. "What's the matter?"

"First of all, Peter will be with his folks, Mr. and Mrs. Taggart."

"No, he wrote me they were going to the country and Peter won't have the time to go that far."

"Well, we just can't afford to have folks to dinner, that's what's the matter." Noella's voice was sharp. "We're not having any turkey this Thanksgiving."

"No turkey?"

"Where do you think we can get money to buy turkey?"

Chubby scribbled absently over his unfinished school work. His pride was wounded and he felt ashamed. "I thought it would be all right to ask Peter."

"You got no right to go around inviting people to dinner without telling me first."

Noella stamped hurriedly through the room, mumbling something unintelligible about "white folks" and "style" and "an upset house."

Chubby stared after her, biting his pencil in perplexity. This was his mother's bad night. On Tuesdays, she was always a bit impatient. That was because she had to wax the extra offices in the Dowling Building. It was a job she had worked at for over four years. Leaving the house at half past nine, she scrubbed all through the night (and waxed on Tuesdays) when most other fellows' mothers were asleep. It was a rotten job, according to Chubby's standards, paying only eleven dollars a week. But it was the best his mother could get.

Noella returned to the room in another flurry of mumblings. Before she left, she said, "See that Jean gets her medicine."

"All right."

Then she was gone.

The sound of her feet descending the stairs brought Chubby back to reality. The questions raced through his mind. What was he going to tell Peter? How was he going to call off this Thanksgiving dinner without revealing the bitter and mortifying truth? Turkeys on Thanksgiving were traditional. They were the accepted, expected, and necessary item. Thanksgiving without a turkey just wasn't Thanksgiving.

Then Chubby frowned and remembered the word—Depression.

Chubby did not quite understand the Depression. According to the talk and the newspapers it was something that was started either by underconsumption or overproduction. Old Sam Cooper blamed it on a senate that was anti-business, but most of the men around Harlem blamed it on a system that was anti-labor. Stocks and bonds, bull and bear markets, and protective tariffs were a lot of other things Chubby could not quite grasp, either. But the things he did understand were these: the longer lines outside the relief offices, the stale bread that his mother was buying more frequently (five cents a loaf at Ward's if it was two days old), the butterfish in place of meat, and the holes in his own shoes.

This was the Depression.

Chubby walked to the front room and looked southward over the packed and cluttered maze of brick and concrete that was Harlem. The acrid smoke of burning wood from a fire on the street below made his nose wrinkle. The boys were roasting potatoes down there in the street, potatoes pinched

The Foundling

from the vegetable wagons and interstate trucks. Up the street, three fellows were tossing a football under the light of a lamp post. They were laughing. Then he saw his mother walking quickly along the street toward the subway. She was late tonight. She was hurrying. Chubby watched her until she turned the corner.

"I got to do something about that Thanksgiving dinner," Chubby breathed to himself. "Just got to do something." He sighed then and walked back to the kitchen. The small brown bottle was on the shelf.

"Jean."

"Yes?"

"Medicine."

The girl walked into the kitchen and sat on a chair. Her hands were folded in her lap, and though she was eighteen, the patient expression in her eyes made Chubby think of her as a mere child.

"Open your mouth, Jean. This is going to make you strong."

The girl swallowed the medicine from the spoon.

"It's good for me?"

"You bet, Jean."

"Can I stay with you in the kitchen?"

"Sure. Do you like magazines, Jean?"

"Yes."

"Want to see something nice?"

"Yes."

"Okay. I'll show you page seven."

Page seven was Chubby's dream. There was no reason in

The Foundling

the world, according to page seven, why he, George Sands, should not become the world's greatest electrical engineer, carpenter, radio technician, mechanic, or public accountant. It was stated there emphatically on page seven.

"See that, Jean?" He read the big black letters for her.

America Affords You Unlimited Opportunities ! ! ! ACT NOW ! ! !

Study These Courses In Your Own Home ! ! !

"Isn't that something, Jean?"

"Yes."

Chubby sensed that Jean did not fully comprehend the drift of his dreaming, but it was consoling merely to talk out loud about his plans for the future.

"Electrical engineers are important people, Jean."

The girl laughed softly.

"Public accountants are something, too."

Chubby was secretly gratified at this forward-looking attitude he was developing towards life. "That's the trouble with folks like us, Jean. We don't get ready for the future. Why, in five or six years, I'll be making enough money for you, Mom, and me to live in a nice house. Would you like to live in a house with a lawn around it . . . your very own house?"

Jean laughed vaguely.

"We can get us some big soft chairs like those in the store windows. Blue plush ones, Jean. And we'll have cups and saucers that match instead of every kind of cups and saucers. And a tea-table, too. Mom would like a tea-table."

"We'll put red roses on the tea-table, huh, George?"

"Real red roses, Jean."

The Foundling

Chubby fingered the seven dollars in his pocket and looked longingly at the litany of advertised American opportunities listed on page seven. Then he sighed. His imagination skipped instantly from tea-tables and plush chairs to the windows at Weisbecker's. Turkeys, in their bluish-whitish skins, were hanging on the hooks at Weisbecker's.

"Jean, do you like turkey?"

"Yes."

Chubby turned in the chair and looked closely at his sister's face. She was staring down at him with her placid, cool, childlike eyes. Her black hair, braided and tied at the ends with frayed bits of blue ribbon, was glistening under the kitchen light. It was easy to dream about Jean for this one magic moment. Page seven in the magazine was better than a fairy tale. It was the wand of an electrical engineer touching Jean's cotton dress to instantaneous white silk. Chubby saw it all so clearly on page seven. Red shoes, real leather ones, were on Jean's feet. She was smiling at him through a mist of expensive-smelling perfume. Her hair was studded with a crescent of pearls, genuine creamy ones—so miraculous was the wand of an electrical engineer.

The dream faded, however, when Chubby's fingers felt the seven dollars in his pocket. The walls of the house came back into gray, depressing focus, and Jean was standing there, clothed in limp, everyday cotton.

"Jean, I guess we can't have everything, can we?"

"Yes."

"No, we can't, Jean. Not everything. Maybe some day we'll have everything. But right now . . ." Chubby stopped abruptly. There was no sense in revealing all his plans to Jean. "Right now, you'd better get some sleep, Jean."

Ten minutes later, Chubby, with the magazine in his hand, walked upstairs to see Sam Cooper. The aged, white-haired Jew was sitting by a stove with a half-finished rose over his knee. Artificial flowers and flat cardboard slats were piled on top of an old piano. Dozens of books, stacked in egg crates, lined the wall.

Ole Sam Cooper was an unusual man, Chubby thought. He was frail and seventy, maybe even eighty; and his face was framed in a snowy beard that fell all the way to his vest. Old Sam had the gentlest eyes, blue and kind; and they looked at you through the thick bifocals, sometimes solemnly, and sometimes with a twinkle far back inside them. His hands, too, were remarkable. Thin, white, and wrinkled with age, they moved nevertheless with a delicacy of precision over the artificial roses—sifting and sorting stems, pinching buds, and rolling the most expert kind of curls into the fringes of the red petals. There was a time, the neighbors said, when old Sam used to work with wax. "Those were mighty sweet wax flowers Sam used to make," old Henrietta declared. "I declare to goodness, you couldn't beat Sam's lilies of the valley. White, and tiny, and pretty! Almost bustin' into real perfume!" But that was in the days when Sam Cooper was younger.

Yes, Sam was an unusual person, Chubby thought, as he stood there facing the aged man. Sam must be intelligent, too. All one had to do was look at the big books he had, enormous books with gold letters on the backs of them. Surely, he must

The Foundling

have been a great man once upon a time. An artist, perhaps. Or a musician (didn't he teach Jean how to sing?) Or maybe even a professor.

"I want to talk to you about something, Sam," Chubby began.

"Sit down, George."

Chubby showed Sam page seven in the magazine and explained the endless possibilities of getting himself educated. "There's a great future in electrical engineering, Sam."

"So?"

"Do you think so?"

"Of course."

"Do you think I ought to specialize in it?"

"Why certainly, son. I think you ought to specialize in anything worthwhile. You're young and you've got your life before you."

"But . . . you see I also . . ." Chubby faltered.

Sam placed the rose on the floor. "Go on, George. Speak."

"I have seven dollars and twenty-five cents saved for this electrical engineering course."

"I see."

"Well . . . Thanksgiving is coming day after tomorrow."

"Yes?"

"Well . . . I was thinking we ought to have a turkey for Thanksgiving."

"Naturally."

"But my mother said she can't afford a turkey . . . and . . ."

Sam must have sensed the dilemma. Sam was a scholar.

The Foundling

"You're thinking about spending that seven dollars for a turkey instead of the electrical engineering course?"

"Well, I don't know." Chubby was thinking about Peter and the present precarious state of the Thanksgiving dinner.

Old Sam Cooper stroked his beard philosophically. "Let me think this out."

"Tell you what, George," he confided, pushing his slipping spectacles into place. "You just forget the electrical engineering course for the present. Go out and buy a turkey for your mother."

"You think I ought to forget the electrical . . .?"

"Come here, George. I want to show you something." The old man removed a frayed wallet from his pocket. His thin, wrinkled fingers trembled as he extracted the faded picture. "Look, George. Hold it to the light."

Chubby studied the portrait, cracked and yellowed with age. "Is this your . . .?"

"My mother, George."

"She looks nice, Mr. Cooper."

"She was a lady, son." The old man rocked back and forth easily, and his black leather slippers with the elastic sides were squeaking in tempo with the chair. There was a distant memory in Sam's eyes, and he spoke as in a revery.

"I still see her standing in the square in Cracow, a shawl over her head. She smiled more proudly that day than ever I remember. She was looking down at me. I was twelve years old. I had run that day . . . run all the way past the Mariecki, up from the market place. And I said to her, 'Look, mother. Figs! I bought a string of dried figs for you.' I said it loudly, in a big voice. And she took the figs, and she reached for my hand, and squeezed my fingers. And my hand was stinging where the blisters were. And she felt the blisters, and said, 'You bought your first figs for me with blisters, son. You bought your first figs with the lumber you lifted out of the Vistula." Sam's eyes clouded and he added, "I was happy that day."

Old Sam's shoes and the rocker squeaked in slow, rhythmic punctuation. "Yes, George. It's something I can't forget. I'll always remember that the sweetest hour of my life was the shining of my mother's face looking at me in the market place in Cracow."

Chubby shifted uneasily. "Dried figs?"

"You get to like dried figs in Poland, George."

But Chubby Sands was slightly mystified.

Then old Sam Cooper wheezed a sigh. "No, George. Don't worry about that electrical engineering course right now. Buy your mother a turkey." The old man placed the picture back into his wallet. Then his voice shook. "I wish it could have been turkey instead of dried figs . . . for her."

Chubby took a deep breath. This solemnity made him uneasy. "I figured on a turkey myself, Sam."

So the problem was solved for Chubby. Actually, it was as he had wanted it. It would come as a pleasant surprise to his hard-working, floor-waxing mother. To heck with page seven. Thanksgiving was going to be a big, jolly, cranberryish, gravy-with-giblets, and jug-of-cider affair. Peter, his best friend, would be there to enjoy it, too.

Chubby smiled broadly. "Thanks, Mr. Cooper."

The Foundling

"Don't mention it."

"By the way," Chubby felt himself lifted and carried on a tidal wave of prodigality, "would you like to have your Thanksgiving dinner with us?"

Sam coughed with distinction. "Well, I was considering a light luncheon with . . . er . . ." he hesitated.

Chubby's young heart understood the pride of a dignified but penniless old man.

"We'll have lots of turkey, Mr. Cooper."

"Thank you, George. I believe I . . . well, yes. I'll be very pleased to join you."

At four o'clock on the following day, Chubby walked buoyantly westward on 125th Street. It was Thanksgiving Eve. Under his left arm, he carried Dooley's *First Principles of Algebra,* Hedgewood's *Exercises in English,* Goudy's *American History,* and a fifteen-cent copy of *Dick* [Frank's younger brother] *Merriwell.* Under his right arm, he carried an eight-pound turkey, cleaned and wrapped in Weisbecker's marble-colored paper, two pounds of brilliant, red cranberries, a half-dozen stalks of celery, eight yams, and a small box of spice. "This'll knock Mom for a loop," he chuckled. "She's going to be real happy when she sees this turkey."

By some mysterious turn in the tides of human affairs, Mrs. Noella Anderson Sands was not exactly happy that afternoon. She was startled and momentarily upset.

"What you got in those packages, George?"

"Turkey and stuff."

"Turkey!"

The Foundling

"Yes. I saved the money for it," Chubby explained.

"But I already bought a turkey myself."

The news fell like a hammer on Chubby's complacency. "You bought a turkey, too?"

" 'Course, I did. You said you were inviting people."

"But, I thought you said . . ."

The issue became a turmoil of apologies and explanations. In the midst of the confusion, a knock sounded at the door.

"Come in," Mrs. Sands said.

The door opened and Peter Lane was standing at the threshold with a straw basket under his arm.

"Hello, Peter," Chubby laughed. "Come in."

"Excuse me, I won't be staying long," Peter said. "Just brought you a little present from Father Duane and the Mount."

"Present?"

"It's a turkey, Chub. Jim Randall picked it out himself. Must be a twenty-pounder at least."

Noella's eyes popped in amazement. "But we already got . . ." Then she collapsed in a chair. She was shaking with loud and uncontrolled laughter. "No, I never saw the like. Three turkeys for Thanksgiving!"

Chubby ran his fingers through his close, kinky hair. "Can you imagine that, Peter? We got three turkeys."

At that moment, old Henrietta entered the room. "What's all the excitement about?" she asked with a curious twinkle in her eye.

Noella tried to explain. "Henrietta, we got three . . ." but she rippled into another rolling wave of laughter.

The Foundling

"We got three turkeys for tomorrow," Chubby explained.

"*Three!*" Henrietta exclaimed. Then drawing herself up to the solemnity of the occasion, and in a voice that could be heard clear to Eighth Avenue, she declared, "Glory be to God, and great day in the morning, folks! Looks like we hit the jack pot!"

Later that evening, after Peter had left, Noella Anderson said, "We've got plenty to eat, George. More than enough. Three, big, tender turkeys. So let's share with some of the folks."

"We could invite Abel Ames, Mom."

"Sure. And Bobby, the janitor. He'd like it."

Noella smiled at Chubby. "This is going to be a good Thanksgiving, George."

The table was set, accordingly, for that memorable Thursday. Old Henrietta was there at three o'clock, bubbling with geniality in her purple Sunday dress. Then came the janitor, Bobby Jennings, together with his wife and the three-year-old twins, Arthur and Alice. Next came Abel Ames, a tall, gaunt gentleman harassed with the weight of domesticity, which included a wife and four girl-cherubs dressed in brown jumpers.

"How are things, Abel?" Noella shouted, as she emerged through the steam of the kitchen.

"I'm doin' okay, Noella," the thin man answered. And because the caraway and raisins and thyme were thick in the festive air, he laughed from the depths of his hungry heart—and stomach, "Doggone, Noella, I'm awfully happy to be here today."

Old Henrietta roared and slapped the fragile man on the back.

Then the youngest Ames, a frizzly-headed youngster, squeaked in a timid but rehearsed voice: "Happy T'anksgivin', everbuddy!"

At which the beaming Henrietta stooped and lifted the frightened child in her arms. "I declare to goodness, you're a real honey lamb, ain't you?"

At which the proud Mrs. Ames smiled and congratulated Henrietta for looking younger than ever.

To which Henrietta replied that it was nothing but a good conscience and a hearty appetite that kept her "pert as a spring chicken."

Then the doorbell rang.

Peter Lane entered. He was momentarily at a loss before all the company.

"This way, Peter," Chubby shouted.

There was a quick exchange of introductions, with Chubby and Noella escorting Peter from the dining room to the kitchen.

"Some crowd, huh, Chub?" Peter asked.

"I guess almost everybody's here," Chubby answered.

But it wasn't until old Sam Cooper arrived, dressed in a black coat and striped trousers, that the party got under way. Jean Sands was holding the old man's hand. They were standing in the doorway, and the cheer that went up at their arrival left the youngest Ames child clinging frantically to her mother's dress.

Twenty minutes later, they were gathered around the two

tables. The feast was about to begin. Noella was standing next to Chubby, when she said, "You're the man of the house, son. Say the grace."

"All right, Mom." While the guests bowed their heads, Chubby prayed quietly: "Bless us, O Lord, and these Thy gifts which we are about to receive from Thy bounty, through Christ Our Lord, Amen."

"Amen," Henrietta repeated.

"Amen," Abel Ames re-echoed.

"Just a minute, folks." It was old Sam, rising slowly to his feet. Jean was looking at him with wide wonderment in her eyes.

"Shush, Arthur," Mrs. Jennings cautioned.

"Quiet, everybody," Henrietta said. "Sam's goin' to say somethin'."

The room fell into silence.

"This isn't a speech, folks," Sam began. "I only want to say something that's been on my mind for . . . oh . . . maybe twenty . . . maybe thirty years." He ran his trembling fingers through his beard. "I guess people all over New York City are sitting down today eating turkey. All over these United States, they're sitting around tables . . . like us . . . enjoying something to eat . . . and . . . and thanking God for it."

"Shush, Arthur!" Mrs. Jennings said to her little son, squirming in the high chair.

"Well," continued old Sam Cooper, "I'd like to tell you what I'm thankful for . . . I'm thankful for people like you . . . kind people . . . neighbors . . . simple, fun-loving people with whom I share the joys of this day. And I'm thankful to God for giving me this home here in Harlem with you . . . where I can live, and move and . . . and spend my days in peace."

The old man's voice was faltering, and his eyes were getting misty and more kind. "That's what I wanted to say. That's what I'm thankful for . . . for peace. The peace of walking to the corner, to the store, to the park, to my synagogue, and back again to home. That's what America means to me and I'm thankful for it. I'm thankful for every day I've had the privilege to live, and I'm thankful for the many days I've lived in this country. I'm thankful for this, especially this great honor . . . the kindest honor that you could bestow on me, which is the invitation to sit down with you at your table. And to God Who is the Father of us all . . . Black and White . . . Whose Name I have tried to honor in my kiddush cups and in the talith that my mother smiled to see around my shoulder. To the good God of Israel, I offer on this happiest of days my sincere thanks."

"Amen," Abel Ames breathed.

"Amen," Henrietta added.

"And now, folks, I have very little to offer . . . except this." Old Sam lifted a brown paper package from the seat. "It's not much." He opened the package slowly, carefully. "It's a token of my esteem."

"Lilies of the valley!" Henrietta exclaimed. "Your best wax flowers, Sam!"

"Yes, my best flowers." Sam was smiling proudly.

The guests applauded loudly; Peter Lane was grinning at

The Foundling

Chub; Noella was the triumphant matron; even Jean Sands was smiling happily; and old Henrietta, in a voice that carried out of the rooms and across the street, declared, "Sam, these flowers are just bustin' with real perfume!"

And Chubby thought it was good and fitting that the turkeys should be brought in then, steaming hot and golden, and placed appropriately near the white-flower gift of a poor but grand old man.

Chapter 18

THE YEARS passed at Mount Mary with the interminable routine of classes and manual labor. The summers, heralded always by the high piping of frogs and the gay galloping of heifers turned loose from the barn, were getting even more glorious for Peter.

He was twenty!

He was a man, now, working at Mount Mary as an assistant to Jim Randall, the foreman.

"If you want to stay here at the Mount, Peter, we'll be glad to have you," Father Duane had said that day, three years ago. "It's about time we put you on the payroll."

"I'd like to stay, Father. Besides, those music lessons with Sister Crescentia . . ."

The priest laughed. "Is that all you ever talk about, music?"

Peter grinned happily. "It's great stuff, Father."

The Foundling

Sister Crescentia had continued to supervise Peter's organ lessons with tireless precision. She had been more than gracious during the past year, and Peter noted that her interruptions were less frequent, now. When he turned on the organ bench to listen to her criticism, her eyes would invariably be closed and she would phrase the words in a voice that was scarcely above a whisper.

Then came the night in the organ loft when this nun, sitting near Peter with her white face caught partly in the gleam of the music lamp, smiled wearily and said something which even then sounded like a premonition. The church was still vibrating with the rondo finale that had come up from a minor and concluded on a D major.

"Play that last passage again, Peter."

The organ, gathering itself hungrily in the minor like a great live thing, burst forth once more with all the tonal satisfaction of the triumphant resolution.

Sister Crescentia looked at Peter and her lips quivered. "There's nothing more beautiful than ending on the major, is there, Peter?" It was the way she said it that made him remember the sentence. *"There's nothing more beautiful than ending on the major."* She rose slowly then and gave him the keys for the first time in three years. "You lock it up tonight, Peter."

"Yes, Sister."

She paused to look at him through the spokes of the spiral stairway. "Good night, Peter."

"Good night, Sister."

Two days later, Father Duane broke the news to Peter.

The Foundling

"Sister Crescentia is a very sick woman. She has tuberculosis, Peter. You will please keep that to yourself. I'm telling you this because . . . well, I know how much you think of her." The old priest puffed on his pipe slowly. "I have another reason also. Sister Crescentia wants to stay here until the eighth of September. That's a week from now. It's also the twenty-eighth anniversary of her vows." Father Duane stared thoughtfully at the ceiling. "She's spent twenty-three of those years right here at Mount Mary. That's a long time, isn't it?"

Peter agreed.

"And it wouldn't be right to let her go without showing her some little sign of appreciation. On the morning of the eighth, therefore, before we take her to New York, we will have a High Mass. I'll say a few words, and we'll have all the children sing. Then here's where you come in. Before the Mass starts, I want you to play an organ recital, or concert, or whatever you call those things. Something nice and short."

"I'll be glad to, Father."

"She'll appreciate it, Peter. I know she will."

Peter rose to leave.

"And don't breathe a word of it to anybody. We want to surprise her, remember."

"I'll remember."

It was difficult to make himself believe that Sister Crescentia was ill. Only the day before, he had seen her taking those long, quick strides over the road to Saint John's. In the numerous activities at the Mount, she seemed always to maintain a composure that defied any compromise with human frailty.

The Foundling

The night before the eighth of September, Peter was sitting at the organ practicing the "surprise" recital when Sister Crescentia climbed the spiral stairway. Her face was drawn and tired.

Her first question was startling. "Are you practicing an organ recital in my honor, Peter?"

All Father Duane's plans were shattered at one stroke. For a few seconds, Peter made incoherent attempts to conceal the facts, but she smiled wearily and said, "It's all right, Peter. I know all about what's going on." Then she sat in the chair and folded her hands. "You may begin, Peter."

"You want me to play the selections *now*?"

"Yes. After twenty-eight years in religious life, I think I have the privilege of choosing my own recital." Merriment was shining in her dark eyes. "Besides, I'm curious to know what you've selected."

So Peter played for her—his first selection for an organ recital. He had passed over Handel and Bach. He had passed over Franck and Gounod. Instead, he had chosen the saddest and most beautiful singer of songs, Franz Schubert.

The great pipes of the organ towered to the window, and seemed for an instant to stand in tall silhouettes like some far forest, breathing a deep music-prayer to the world. As the strains of that *Ave Maria* filled the darkened church, Peter knew somehow that this tired, sick nun was more beautiful than the music he was playing. She was more than the sadness and tenderness of Schubert. At that moment, her closed eyes and pale features reminded him of a picture he had seen somewhere under a Cross.

The Foundling

When he finished, she opened her eyes, and he saw that she had been crying. She smiled and rose from her chair. "Thank you, Peter, if you play nothing else tomorrow, that *Ave Maria* will be enough."

She walked down the spiral stairway and paused when her head was just above the level of the floor. "God bless you, Peter."

A Special Delivery letter arrived at Mount Mary on a blustery March morning.

"Still getting mail, eh, Peter?" Jim Randall swung the reins in his hand. The horses were eager to start for the north field.

"Yeah, Sister Crescentia keeps writing ever since she went to Gabriel's. She's been writing steady for over two months, now."

For Sister Crescentia, the letter was more concise than usual. She wrote:

"I want you to come to see me right away if you can. Sister Felicia will give you the train fare. Show her this letter and she will understand."

Peter had money of his own, so he did not show the letter to Sister Felicia. When he was purchasing the ticket at Grand Central that morning, he realized suddenly that Sister Crescentia had not written the letter herself.

"Here's your change, sir," the man said.

Peter was studying the letter as he lifted the ticket and money from the counter. It was not Sister Crescentia's hand that had written the lines, and he knew that something was seriously wrong.

When Peter entered the small room of the convalescent home that evening, Sister Crescentia was smiling.

"Hello, Peter," she said.

"Hello, Sister." He had difficulty concealing the shock at seeing her lying helpless in bed. How different and utterly human she looked, now that she was without her black serge religious garb.

"Sit down, Peter." Her long white fingers reached out to his hand. "You came quickly."

"You told me to come right away, Sister."

She stared at the ceiling for a long time, and Peter suspected that she was happy; but it was very difficult to read Sister Crescentia's thoughts.

"I can't eat bananas now, Peter. I thought that was so very good of you to send me bananas, parcel post. Did you know that I liked bananas?"

"No, Sister."

She asked him then about his music, and her eyes gleamed when he described Beethoven's *Ninth Symphony*.

"Did you know that he wrote that when he was deaf?" she asked.

"No, I didn't, Sister."

"Well, he did."

A loud-speaker in the hall was calling for a doctor, and when it quieted, Sister Crescentia turned her head on the pillow and faced Peter. She spoke very slowly, which was wholly unlike her. "I don't know how to begin, Peter, except to say that I wanted to see you once more. I want you to know that I am grateful for all the afternoons and evenings of all the years you have devoted yourself to your music. To see you develop day by day made me more happy than you'll ever guess. I'm sure there were times when I was too cross and exacting with you. But I know you'll forgive me, because I've always had the highest ambitions for you."

Peter tried to assure her that he had never found her too cross or exacting. Sister Crescentia smiled.

"I'm quite selfish also, Peter," she added. "So selfish that I'm going to surprise you." She waited for a few seconds, and then she said, "See that box on the table?"

"Yes, Sister."

"Open it."

He opened it and found reams of orchestration written in ink. "It's music, Sister Crescentia."

"Yes, it's music." Her eyes were extremely tired. "You're the first one who has ever seen that music."

The story unfolded hesitantly. It was an odd and simple story, but wondrously beautiful from the lips of the nun.

"Would you be surprised if I told you that I wanted to write a symphony?" she asked.

"No, Sister. I'm sure you could write a symphony if you wanted to."

Amusement was creeping into the corners of her eyes. "Really, it's the truth. I did want to write a symphony. I wanted to write it when I was twelve years old; not in music at first, but in words . . . in a flood of words I was too young to write. Mind if I tell you about it?"

"No, Sister."

"Well, it began under a bridge. It began under a bridge, one day, when I saw several boys beating a little fellow. Perhaps I shouldn't have been too surprised. It happened around our neighborhood often. Fights, I mean. I had heard of brutality—especially this kind. I suppose there were some people who were used to it. But I was twelve years old at the time, Peter, and I wasn't used to it. It was horrible and frightening. I screamed that day and ran all the way home. I couldn't forget the sound of their fists beating against the head and body of that small boy. For days and months I couldn't get that sight out of my mind. When I went to bed that first night, I heard the water dripping in the sink. It's so clear to me, Peter. I must have been feverish because every drop of that water seemed to get louder and louder, beating like so many fists against a little boy. It was then that I had a strange longing to go back under the bridge and find him. I wanted to take him in my arms and put ointments and all the softest, whitest cotton on his face."

Sister Crescentia paused and looked at Peter as if she almost suspected that he was doubting her words. "It's the truth, Peter. I wanted to do all this. More than anything else, I wanted to carry that little boy from the bridge, carry him through the streets so all the people could see him. It was my favorite dream. I saw all the people coming out of the houses, out of the tenements and apartments. They were kind people, and when I passed by they placed their hands tenderly on the head of my boy. And best of all, under the bridge, I found the boys who had beat him. And even they,

Peter, even *they* came forward and placed their hands on the head of my boy. And always . . ." Sister Crescentia was looking at the ceiling as she added, "and always I would say to them in this dream of mine, 'That's not enough. It's not enough to place your hand on his head. You must take him in your arms.'"

A dog howled somewhere and Peter felt suddenly chilled and lonely in the cool mountain air that filled the room.

"I think that was my first call to become a nun, Peter. All my life I wanted to . . . well, to find people under bridges and help them." She smiled quickly. "It was wonderful helping the children at Mount Mary, who had been found under some bridge or another, but you were lucky, Peter," she added, "you were already in a crib when you were found!"

Sister Crescentia asked for the water that was on the table and, after sipping a few drops, she closed her eyes. "And that also is the reason why I wanted to write a symphony. It was an odd notion, but perhaps not too odd, for I have found a language of suffering and sympathy and joy in music that . . ." She breathed deeply and did not finish the sentence. Her eyes were dreamy and she spoke very slowly. "It was to be a grand symphony, Peter, full of the sunshine of God's creation. That was the first movement. It would be wide as the earth with God moving on the hills and over the waters.

She continued, "The second movement, the andante, was to be under an old and gloomy bridge. It was to be heavy with the sadness of sin and violence. And because I heard it in the dark key of C Minor, it was to be almost hopeless, a sort of trembling on edges of despair." She remained quiet for a long time. Then she said in a voice that was scarcely above a whisper, "Even a nun must be on guard against despair, Peter."

Her mood was almost gay as she continued. "That's how I heard the third movement of my symphony, Peter. I wanted it to be full of the merry babbling of small children playing in brooks of bubbling clarinets, and I wanted horns blowing lightly, nosegays of music, sprouting quickly like tulips and crocuses growing outside all the classrooms of the world. Do you understand?"

"Yes, Sister."

Sister Crescentia laughed softly. "You never did care much for school, Peter."

He confessed he hadn't.

For the third movement, I wanted the scherzo of childhood, rippling with staccatos of innocence, and Aladdin lamps, and Guardian Angels. I wanted it to sparkle with play and with spirit." She turned and smiled at him. "A piccolo is good at playing hide-and-seek with strings, don't you think, Peter?"

Sister Crescentia looked towards Peter and then at the box on the table. "It's all there, Peter. Those three movements are in the box, and it took me five years to do them. But as yet I haven't written the finale."

"In a little while you'll be able to finish it, Sister. Perhaps a month, maybe two months, and you'll be able to . . ."

But her weary face denied the words he said. "That's why

The Foundling

I wanted you to come, Peter. I want you to finish our symphony."

The calm directness of her voice confused him for a moment. This invitation to write a fourth movement for a symphony was given as easily as she might have directed him to play a piano piece from Hanon. But the startling realization that he had never studied orchestration brought Peter back to reality.

"I'm sorry, Sister, but I don't know how to write for . . ."

"You will, Peter," she interrupted easily. "You'll be able to write. Some day you will. And you'll be able some day to put into that fourth movement all I wanted to say in music."

She outlined it, with her face glowing visibly under her words. "You will lift it out of the despair of that andante. You will take it out of that pizzicato of fists and violence and wickedness. It will come back with the love of God in it, sweeping out over all the earth again in harmonies of light and mercy. It will sing a song of peace for you, Peter, where there will be no crying under bridges, but only love of man for man, and all men for God. There will be nothing more beautiful than ending on *that* major, Peter."

Nothing more beautiful than ending on that major! Peter remembered the words she had spoken long ago in the organ loft.

Sister Crescentia's eyes were glistening when she turned on the pillow and faced him. "Will you do that for me, Peter?"

"I'll do it, Sister. I'll try my best."

She grew tired then and relaxed.

The Foundling

The next morning, shortly before he left, Sister Crescentia opened a prayer book and handing Peter a small yellow leaflet, she said, "This is a prayer my mother used to say. I've read it many times during these past twenty or thirty years. And because it's a blessing, an old Irish mother's blessing, I'll give it to you, the way she gave it to me before I left home."

She was looking out the window when she said the words, exactly as they were written on the leaflet; and her voice never faltered until she came close to the end.

"*May the blessing of Light be on you, light without and light within. May the blessed sunlight shine on you and warm your heart till it glows like a great peat fire, so that the stranger may come and warm himself at it, and also a friend.*

"*And may the light shine out of the two eyes of you like a candle set in two windows of a house, bidding the wanderer to come in out of the storm.*

"*And may the blessing of the Rain be on you—the soft, sweet rain. May it fall upon your spirit so that all the little flowers may spring up, and shed their sweetness on the air.*

"*And may the blessing of the Great Rains be on you; may they beat upon your spirit and wash it fair and clean, and leave there many a shining pool where the blue of heaven shines reflected, and sometimes a star.*

"*And may the blessing of the Earth be on you—the great round earth; may you ever have a kindly greeting for them you pass as you're going along the roads. May the earth be soft under you when you lay out upon it, tired at the end of the day, and may it rest easy over you, when, at the last, you lay out under it; may it rest so lightly over you, that your soul may be quickly through it, and up, and off, and on its way to God."*

A month later, Sister Crescentia died.

They carried her body southward on the rumbling train that skirts the Hudson River. They placed her gently and reverently in the Motherhouse between two rows of brown candles.

People paid their respects that night. All kinds of people. They came into the chapel and knelt beside the quiet figures of the nuns.

Peter Lane also paid his respects. He couldn't quite formulate the words that came crowding into his prayer. He genuflected quickly and left the chapel.

Outside, in the black night, he looked back at the Motherhouse. It was a quick look. But in that instant when he glanced back at the windows where the brown candles were gleaming, all the kindness and sacrifice of one nun rushed across the years to him. For a moment, he thought he saw her pale face smiling at him from a clump of matted vines. For a moment, he thought he heard an organ playing.

"O good Jesus Christ . . ." he choked. It was a strangled prayer. Then turning and walking down the road from the Motherhouse, Peter Lane cried and prayed for the soul of Sister Crescentia: "Eternal rest, grant unto her, O Lord. Let perpetual light shine upon her!"

Chapter 19

IT WAS a nipping, bright afternoon in November and Peter was actually breathless with the news. The letter was between his fingers, with the pink ticket jutting out of it. He was reading the letter again to make sure this was no mere dream:

". . . and Helen Spalding asked me to go, since I have never seen Notre Dame and Army play, except of course in the newsreels. So there will be Mr. and Mrs. Spalding, Helen and myself in the box.

"Now for the surprise! The extra ticket is for you. Helen thought it would be nice if you also could see the game. If you can't use it, send me a telegram and I'll let the Spaldings know. We are arriving at La Guardia Airport Saturday morning at eleven o'clock. This letter is quite rushed, so please excuse me.

"As ever,
"Barbara."

There it was in Barbara's writing. He was reading the golden sentence for the fifth time. "Helen thought it would

The Foundling

be nice if you also could see the game." Helen Spalding was coming all the way to New York and she was going to occupy the very same box with Peter (including, of course, Mr. and Mrs. Spalding, and Barbara).

So life for Peter began at twenty. Helen would be coming to him on the silver wings of an airplane, and he would be there to greet her when she stepped out of the plane. In the meantime, it was necessary to see Jim Randall.

"I want to borrow your car, Jim."

"All right, Peter."

Ellen Taggart gave him luncheon that day and suggested which stores he should visit. She also offered him money, but he almost proudly refused. So now Peter was driving up Madison Avenue in search of the shoe store that displayed those burnished, bronze-toned, Scotch-grained oxfords with the thick laces. It was a shoe that smacked of the rugged masculinity of college campuses.

"Six dollars and sixty cents, sir," the salesman said.

But what were six dollars and sixty cents now that Helen Spalding was scheduled to arrive on Saturday morning?

Next, he was driving down Lexington Avenue in search of *that* tie. It was to be a conservative maroon, and it must breathe the cool flame of the autumnal sunsets one sees over Fordham or Notre Dame. He had imagined such ties on the men who sit in the shadow of ivy walls, with great big text books under their arms, and great big varsity letters on their chests. And he found it. And furthermore, it had a yellow silk lining.

"One dollar and fifty cents, sir."

A paltry sum indeed for the pleasure of wearing it on Saturday.

The drone of the engines was in his pulse as the plane swung in gradual descent to the runway at La Guardia. It turned slowly and taxied to the pavilion.

Then the door of the plane opened.

In a way, the rest of that Saturday made little difference to Peter. The roar of thousands of football fans in the stands as the players came rushing out on the field, the banners flying, people cheering, bands playing, the final shot of the time-keeper's gun that sent the Irish home to South Bend with another victory under their helmets—all these were boisterous incidentals compared to that moment at La Guardia Airport. It was a lightning interval in which he saw her among the passengers that alighted from the plane.

"Hello, Noodles," she laughed.

It was Barbara Ross grown to the glowing beauty of a woman. It was Barbara as he had never dreamed she might be, with provocative amusement in her voice.

"I said hello, Noodles," Barbara repeated.

"Hello, Barbara," Peter gasped.

"Aren't you going to say hello to Helen?"

"Oh, hello, Helen."

That's how it was. Peter's young world, built on a memory of jelly beans, lard, lemons, and Helen Spalding dissolved instantaneously under the smile of a girl who said "Noodles." Time was a magic element that took the braids of fifteen-year-old Barbara Ross and shook them in lustrous dark glory over the shoulders of womanhood.

Peter bemoaned his luck that night in the quiet of his bungalow at Mount Mary. "And to think she used to come riding after me on a bike with her braids in the wind! Why didn't I appreciate her before this? Why didn't I send Barbara a box of candy or something during all these years?"

Barbara was leaving for Boston with the Spaldings the next day, and, perhaps, he would never see her again. She had to be back for classes at Emmanuel College where she was majoring in science. That was a disturbing fact. Higher education in Boston. Those sleek college men who went to the Massachusetts Institute of Technology, Holy Cross, Harvard, Boston College, and University and a host of other New England institutions, were probably proposing marriage to Barbara from one end of the academic year to the other. It was a depressing picture he drew that night, replete with handsome sophomores, juniors, seniors, crew hair cuts, flashing roadsters, briar pipes, and flat New England accents. "You'd probably have to get at least a Ph.D. to land a girl like Barbara," he moaned. And here he was at Mount Mary, supervisor of the farm with an unfinished symphony in his hands and the stains of carrot juice still on his fingers. His maroon tie, viewed in the distorted mirror, looked less impressive now. Even the bronze-toned shoes appeared to be less suggestive of the debonair dash of the American campus.

In the silence of that November night, sitting in the wicker rocker, Peter caught the first sharp lesson of a truth one learns inevitably with the passage of time. "I'm getting older, I guess," he admitted to himself. He would be twenty-one in December.

The Foundling

He was thinking of a small Italian woman he had seen kneeling one day before a row of vigil lights. It was in a church on one of the side streets of New York, and the simple faith of the woman was something he could not forget. The quiet pleading was visible in her face as she looked upward to the altar. And watching her that day, he remembered the words of old Father Duane. "God is interested in the meat, bread, salt, and butter that you put on your table. He's interested in the crimp that gets into a man's back. He's interested in anything you've got to say to Him, simply because He's God."

Simply because He's God.

"I'm getting older, I guess," he repeated later that night as he knelt in the dark of the church. It was a good way to begin a prayer, he thought.

"I'm getting older, Lord, and I might as well admit it. Maybe I shouldn't figure too much on flashy shoes and ties. Maybe I shouldn't bank too much on clothes and stuff, although one does have to dress up a bit these days. Anyway," the faith of a small Italian woman was encouraging him, "anyway, I know You must be interested in us. You're interested in the meat, and bread, and other things we put on the table. You're interested even in sparrows." This was a momentary and inspired digression. "So you must be interested even more in people, including myself and . . . well, Barbara."

He was sure he was in love with Barbara. Just one look at her today at La Guardia Airport and . . . well, she was as nice as anyone he had ever seen. And he knew she was good because he could see it in her eyes. "She's certainly wonderful," he said, "and I can't help hoping that some day she will marry me."

At ten o'clock the next morning, the knock came at Peter's door. The fourth page of a letter he was going to send to Barbara was still wet with the ink when he heard her voice.

"Are you there, Noodles?"

It was Barbara Ross.

"I thought I'd see you once more before I go back. We're leaving on the five o'clock for Boston this afternoon," she said, swinging her handbag in the doorway.

"Did you come all the way to Mount Mary by yourself?"

"Yes. The Spaldings are seeing friends."

"Well, come in, Barbara," he said in a voice that trembled a little.

She sat in the wicker rocker and removed her hat. "So *this* is where you live."

"Yes. It's a bit out of the way, but I like it up here near the ice house."

"You even have a fireplace."

"Jim Randall put that in two years ago."

"And heaps of logs."

"Plenty of logs, Barbara."

It went on like that in casual pleasantries. Peter told her how, four years ago, Father Duane had let him have the old run-down bungalow for his very own, how he and Jim Randall had repaired it and made it snug, and how Father Duane let him borrow one of the Mount's pianos so he

The Foundling

could practise whenever he had the time. And while he talked, he could not help recalling all the hours he had spent here thinking and dreaming of—of all people—Helen! How absurd it was now. It seemed to him that one Peter was talking easily and simply about life at the Mount and another, the real Peter, was hovering nearby eager to put an end to this nonsense and get down to the business of the day—telling Barbara that he thought she was the loveliest creature who had ever sat in a wicker chair.

"You have quite a big institution here," Barbara interrupted.

"Yes, Barbara. More than fifteen hundred here now."

"And you're the big farmer on the property?"

"Not too big. Just drawing down steady pay, supervising the help."

"Almost six feet of you, I'd say."

"Five feet eleven, Barbara."

Thus the moments went that morning. It was only after they had had lunch at Jim Randall's, and had walked through the corridors, playgrounds, and workshops at the institution that Peter suggested the road that ran to the stubble field beyond the orchard.

"But will I have time, Peter?"

"Sure you'll have time."

He was placing a wild, desperate hope in the clean cedar rails that bordered the field. One might rest one's elbows on one of those rails and look out over the stubble toward the sun. One might say many things to a girl with a cedar rail for support.

The Foundling

She stood there beside him with her coat buttoned tightly against the cold wind.

"Barbara."

"Yes?"

"Do you remember the day long ago when we stood at an old field fence at Bodiou's farm?"

"Yes."

"It seems ages ago. Do you remember what you told me that day, Barbara?"

"I do."

"Something about forks and spoons in a piano."

Barbara was laughing easily. "I was a baby at fifteen."

"Maybe you were. Maybe you weren't. But anyway . . . what I want to say is . . . I wouldn't mind now if you put forks and spoons into the piano."

"No?"

"No."

Her face was turned from him, and he wondered if he had made a mistake. "Barbara, there's something I'd like to tell you."

"Yes."

"I saw someone come out of a crowd at the airport yesterday. She was unlike anything I've ever dreamed. She was beautiful, different, yet she was the same."

"Who was she?"

"Barbara Ross."

A faint smile was on her lips as she faced him. "What in the world are you trying to say, Peter?"

"Couldn't you try to guess?"

"It's time to go," she answered. "You'll see me to the bus now, won't you?"

"I'm seeing you all the way to New York. Jim Randall will let me take his car."

"It's not necessary."

"I'll see you all the way to Boston if you want me to, Barbara."

"It's almost two-thirty, Peter."

"Are you listening to me, Barbara?"

"And the Spaldings will never forgive me if I miss that train!"

"Forget the Spaldings. Will you listen to me?"

"Yes. What do you want?"

"I want you some day to become Mrs. Peter Lane."

There! He had said it more quickly and emphatically than he had ever dreamed of doing. It was better and more conclusive than all the conventional rigmarole and circumlocution. "I want to marry you, Barbara."

Her eyes were studying him in wide surprise. "After seeing me one day in New York, Peter, do you mean to stand there and say . . .?"

"After a thousand days, Barbara, I know I would say it and believe it forever." The blood seemed to be pounding in his ears like thunder.

She began to laugh quietly again. After a short while, she said the phrase that was to flicker like a candle through many a dark night. "Take my hand, Noodles," she said, as they turned and walked back over the road together, over a road which Peter hoped would have no ending.

Chapter 20

WILLIAM SNOGGINS MULROONEY was long past that era of springs wherein a young man's fancy is said to turn to thoughts of love. April spriteliness was in the air that Saturday morning, it was true; and the crocus was lifting its yellow horn; and the robins were on the wing. But outside St. Rita's Church, William Snoggins Mulrooney was roaring like a December storm.

"What's the trouble, Mr. Mulrooney?" the pastor asked.

"Aw, Father, sometimes I'd like to shake 'em out of their boots."

"Shake whom?" asked the pastor with grammatical exactness.

"Those rascally heathens, the altar boys." Snoggins was fanning himself furiously with his derby.

"What did they do now?"

"They're marchin' up and down my waxed floors like a herd of cows."

"Well, why don't you . . .?"

"It's the organist, that Benburston woman, who's at the bottom of it."

"Oh, Miss Benburston!" The pastor studied the sacristan with veiled amusement in his eyes. "What is Miss Benburston up to now?"

"You'd have to be Tom Longboat himself to keep up with her. Processions, processions, processions! She's always rehearsin' for processions. And spoilin' my floors, too."

"The May processions, possibly?"

"I have nothin' against May processions, Father. All honor and glory to the good and lovely Mother of God." Snoggins tipped his derby in genuine reverence. "I have nothin' against May processions. But that Benburston woman, with her dibbin' and dabbin', and her doodin' and dawdin' on that organ; you'd swear the Blessed Mother of God was interested in nothin' but processions!"

"Well, you know how it is with organists, Mulrooney."

"I despise organists!"

"Now, now, Mulrooney. Remember! Love thy neighbor," the pastor counselled as he walked to the rectory.

"Hmph!" Snoggins sniffed. "Love thy neighbor."

Just then, Miss Louise Benburston, the organist, smiled down at Snoggins from the top step of St. Rita's. "Beautiful day, Mr. Mulrooney, isn't it?"

"Rawnph," Mulrooney coughed at her like a bilious lion. He eyed the organist with disdain. Having entered into several disputes with her, Snoggins was only too well aware of this present and proximate occasion of strife. The pastor, himself, had repeatedly insisted in the past that there be more amicable relations between Mr. Mulrooney and Miss Benburston. The pastor insisted, particularly, that Snoggins Mulrooney remember the first and greatest commandment which was *love*. But Snoggins had reminded the pastor with some measure of theological vehemence that he, William Mulrooney, was obliged merely to *love* Miss Benburston, and that nowhere in Holy Scripture could it be shown that he, William Mulrooney, was obliged to *like* the person.

Snoggins growled after the departing organist, "Hmph, Love thy neighbor."

"Hi, Mr. Mulrooney," Paul Taggart shouted from across the street.

"How are you?" Snoggins bellowed back half-heartedly, with a baleful eye still on the departing organist.

The two men shook hands, and traded small talk on the weather.

"Cigar, Mr. Mulrooney?"

"Why, thank you," Mr. Mulrooney beamed. "Nothin' like a smoke to smooth the ruffled edges of the spirit."

"You'll like that cigar."

"How's that boy of ours?" Snoggins asked.

"Peter?"

"Yeah."

"Fine. He's got a new interest in life, Mr. Mulrooney."

"That's so?"

"He's an organist."

"An organist!" Snoggins shuddered instinctively. "Whatever possessed him to become an organist?"

The Foundling

"He likes music."

Snoggins wrinkled his nose, then blew a cloud of smoke. "The world is made of the strangest kind of people, isn't it, Mr. Taggart?"

"As a matter of fact, Peter's going to make a career out of his music."

"That so?" Snoggins blew another cloud of smoke. Then, without blinking an eye, Snoggins asked, "Could Peter use a piano?"

Paul Taggart was perplexed, momentarily. "Well, he has the use of a piano, Mr. Mulrooney. It belongs to the institution out there."

"I mean . . . a piano for himself?"

"Oh!"

"If a fellow's studying to be an organist, he ought to have a piano for himself."

"Yes, I suppose so, Mr. Mulrooney."

"Now, did you ever hear of Jim Delaney, Taggart?"

"No."

"Well, Jim Delaney owns a bar and grill."

"I see."

"Jim's got a piano he wants to get rid of."

"Yes?"

"The customers have been scraping their shins against that piano for the past ten years, Taggart, and Delaney would be a mighty thankful man if we could get it hauled out of there for him."

"I see, Mr. Mulrooney." Paul envisioned the scarred bar and grill instrument. "But do you think that Father Duane would accept . . .? I mean a bar and grill piano, Mr. Mulrooney . . .?"

"What's the matter with a bar and grill piano?"

"Oh . . . nothing I suppose."

"Delaney's as fine a Catholic as ever stepped into a church, and he's got a boy studying for the priesthood, and a girl studying to be . . ."

"I'm not questioning Delaney's character at all, Mr. Mulrooney."

"Tell you what I'll do." Mulrooney flicked his cigar. "Come inside the rectory with me."

Paul Taggart had an uncomfortable feeling of getting involved in something. He was sorry now he had brought up the subject of Peter's music.

In a few minutes, Snoggins Mulrooney had the Rector of Mount Mary on the phone. "Father Duane, this is Mr. William Mulrooney, sacristan of St. Rita's parish."

"Yes, Mr. Mulrooney."

"I'm very interested in one of our boys out there."

"Yes, Mr. Mulrooney."

"Peter Lane."

"Oh, yes, Peter."

"He's a grand boy, Father."

"Yes, Mr. Mulrooney."

"Now, Father, between you and me, would you have any objections to a bar and grill piano?"

The rector hesitated for a moment. After Snoggins succeeded in giving the full details, Father Duane coughed and hedged. "Well, that bar and grill . . ."

"But it's a *good* piano, Father," Snoggins insisted.
"All right, Mr. Mulrooney. I'll take your word."
"Fine!"
"I hope it won't be too much trouble for you, Mr. Mulrooney."
"Aw, Father, I'm an old hand at pianos."

Snoggins flicked an ash off his cigar and wheeled in the office chair like an executive. "Meet me here, Monday night, Taggart," he ordered. "I'm beginning to get an idea."

"Right, Mr. Mulrooney." Paul was too taken aback to offer an objection.

"Yes sir, I got an idea, Taggart," the fat sacristan repeated. A slow smile was coming into his face. "And when Mulrooney gets an idea, *Mulrooney gets an idea!*"

Paul Taggart was suddenly getting sickish. "You're not going to carry that piano in Clancy's funeral coach, are you?"

"Coach!" Snoggins exploded. "Whoever heard of a piano in a funeral coach?"

Paul laughed apologetically. "It's Monday night then, Mr. Mulrooney?"

"At about seven. Yes, I'd say about seven." Mulrooney flicked another cigar ash and took a deep, deep, pleased breath.

Snoggins was an extremely busy man that following Sunday morning. He moved quickly and doggedly through the crowds after the Masses. He peered intently into the eyes of several stalwart pillars of the church; he pleaded, wheedled, gesticulated, and jabbed his stout fingers into their Sunday vests; he held them by the hand, the arm, their coat sleeves,

The Foundling

and even got one gentleman by the suspenders. He spoke to the men of The Holy Name, the Knights of Columbus, and St. Vincent de Paul's. He mopped his brow, raised his eyes heavenwards in supplication, and invariably ended by whispering something about "the poor little, darlin' little orphans."

Paul Taggart was surprised when he came to St. Rita's Monday evening. Snoggins was shouting in the street above the heads of a small, enthusiastic group. People were milling about in confusion with instruments of all sizes in their hands; old cornets, rusty bugles, guitars, mandolins, and accordians. There was something that looked like a tuba, too. But Paul wasn't too sure. It might have been a French horn. There was an old man with a black flute under his arm. There was, also, a lady with a small violin case. And there was a huge victrola.

"Just a minute, folks," Snoggins shouted. "Just a minute. The truck'll be here any time now."

Paul was on the verge of sneaking home when Snoggins spotted him.

"Hello, Taggart," he beamed. "Look what we got for the orphans!"

Paul forced a smile. "Quite a lot of . . . of instruments."

"Those orphans need this kind of stuff, Taggart. Not only Peter. All of them. Somethin' to brighten life for them. Do you remember that parade they had out there years ago?"

"Yes, I do."

"Well, it was a grand parade. But they didn't have enough music. Why, there were kids out there, hundreds of 'em without so much as . . . as a harmonica in their mouths. That's not right, Taggart. Everybody gets an instrument, is my saying!

"*Am I right?*" he roared to the throng.

"Right, Mulrooney!" the group shouted.

Then the truck came. It was a huge, spacious moving van, six-wheeled and impressive with its big hiss of air brakes.

Snoggins ran up to the small driver. "God bless you, Tony. The poor darlin' orphans will never forget this."

Tony D'Ambaglio grinned over the wheel. "Fill 'er up, Mulrooney."

"Right, Tony."

When the last instrument had been packed into the van, Snoggins mounted the tail-board and delivered a short speech.

"This is a great night, tonight, folks. It's a wonderful night for St. Rita's. Your charity is unabounded, friends. It's a hundredfold . . . two hundredfold. And the Good Lord Who said, 'if any man gives a drop of water in my name' . . . that same Good Lord is lookin' down at us tonight, out here in front of St. Rita's, and He's sayin' if any man gives a fiddle or an accordian in My Name, he gives it to Me. And He's sayin', well done thou good and faithful steward."

The slight mix-up of scriptural texts disturbed neither Snoggins nor the smiling parishioners.

"And now, folks, we're off to Delaney's for the piano!" Snoggins exclaimed. "Good-by, everybody."

Paul Taggart climbed beside Snoggins on the van. "Do

The Foundling

you think we'll have any trouble with the instruments, Mr. Mulrooney?"

"Trouble? What kind of trouble?"

"I mean . . . Father Duane is expecting only a piano."

"Well, what difference does it make? Why, we got over ten thousand dollars worth of stuff packed in back of this van that'll knock his eye out," Mulrooney exaggerated grandly. "And let me tell you, Taggart, nobody's kickin' ten thousand dollars around these days. Am I right, Tony?"

The driver grinned behind the wheel. "Right, Mulrooney."

Then they drove to the Bronx where Tony D'Ambaglio's truck pulled up outside Delaney's bar and grill. There was a quick consultation at the rear door with a man in a white apron who took them inside.

The piano was a grayish, soiled object the weight of which Snoggins estimated to be at least two tons. How could they get it out of the grill? Heroic, groaning efforts were made by Paul Taggart, Tony, Snoggins, and two patrons who declared they had been altar boys more than two decades ago, but at the rear door their efforts were balked.

"What's the trouble?" Snoggins demanded, with the sweat pouring off his broad nose.

"You can't squeeze him through the door," Tony explained.

"Is the piano too big?" Snoggins asked.

"No," Tony explained. "The door is too small."

"For the love of God's holy angels and saints," Snoggins exclaimed, "they *got* the piano into this joint. Why can't we get it out?"

The Foundling

One of the patrons who had been an altar boy twenty years ago, wheezed, "Let me figure this thing out."

"Yeah. Let's figure this thing out," the other ex-altar boy panted.

Mr. Delaney, the proprietor, entered at that moment. "What's the trouble, Mulrooney?"

Snoggins collapsed in a chair. He removed his derby and perched it on his knee. "Delaney, where in God's creation did you get a piano like that?"

"What's the matter with it, Mulrooney?"

"It won't go through the door."

Delaney frowned and tightened his lips. "Maybe you've got the wrong angle on it, Mulrooney."

"Angle!" the sacristan snorted. "We've tried all angles. We've jibbed and jabbed and jubbed until . . . well, it's enough to kill an ox."

Delaney circled the piano, studied it, called several of the other patrons in for consultation, measured the door, took a look out into the night, and finally admitted with a sober face, "We've had alterations, Mulrooney."

"Alterations!"

"Yeah. The door used to be two feet wider."

Paul Taggart wanted to laugh, but the agony on Mulrooney's face was too tragic.

"Delaney," Snoggins sighed forlornly, almost bitterly, "Delaney, if you wanted us to bring dynamite, why didn't you tell us?"

"Use your head, Snoggins," said Delaney. "Take it out the front door, that's big enough."

The Foundling

At a quarter of midnight, a large moving van rumbled into Mount Mary. Snoggins was dozing in the seat.

"Where are we?" he asked.

"At the Mount, Mr. Mulrooney."

"Oh."

"We'd better take this stuff to Peter's cabin," Paul suggested.

"By all means," Snoggins agreed. "By all means!"

That night, Paul tried to give an explanation to Peter. "You see, the old man was set on giving instruments to the kids."

"I see," Peter Lane said.

"He wanted to do it for you, Peter," Paul explained. "It started with a piano. You understand?"

"Sure, Paul. I understand. We can still use these instruments. Stop worrying."

"You don't think they'll be any trouble?"

"Not at all."

The moon was shining bright at one o'clock that night at Mount Mary. Three tired men, Tony D'Ambaglio, Paul Taggart, and Peter Lane piled the last of the instruments in the tool shed down by the barn. Snoggins was snoring in the cabin of the van.

Peter laughed. "How did the old fellow ever do it? How did he ever get all these instruments?"

But Paul was tired. He said wearily, "I don't know, Peter. I just don't know how he does it."

They smiled at Snoggins, sprawled on the long black seat of the van in blissful sleep.

PART 4

Chapter 21

ONE MAY morning a month later, Peter Lane opened a letter with eager fingers. It was from Barbara. The very postmark on a letter from Lynnford sent his heart into a flutter. His eyes scanned the lines hungrily, quickly. Then he frowned.

"Lewis," Peter breathed. "It's Lewis again."

Peter sat in a chair and stared at the wall. Why did Barbara keep mentioning Lewis in her letters? Why did she keep writing things like "Lewis called me up last night" and "Lewis and I went to a baseball game"?

This new letter Peter was holding in his hand was creating another wave of suspicion and doubt. Was it jealousy, or anxiety, or what? Peter wasn't sure. He was certain only of one thing—he was in love with Barbara Ross.

Peter read the tragic lines again: "Lewis is such a grand fellow. He came all the way from Newton and took me to the Toll House, yesterday."

The Foundling

Peter began to pace the floor.

Shucks! What was he worrying about? A dinner is a dinner, that's all. Yet, on the other hand, there it was in black and white . . . dinner for two . . . dinner for Barbara and Lewis. Peter didn't like this dinner-for-two business. Why, a fellow could smile and be gracious over a steak for two; he might blow perfect smoke spirals over the salt shakers and say, "You're a wonderful girl, Barbara." That's what dinner for two could lead to. And at the Toll House! Peter bore no malice toward the Toll House, but he found himself wishing that the chef had bungled the job.

On the other hand, Lewis might be perfectly all right. He might be Barbara's second cousin. Peter never thought to ask Barbara.

But Newton! Newton was a long way from Lynnford. What would a fellow from Newton be doing all the way over in Lynnford? They certainly should have good steaks or chops in Newton. Lewis didn't have to travel all the way from Newton to Lynnford for steaks or chops or onion soup.

The twenty-two letters that Barbara had sent during the past four months, stacked tightly in the rubber band on top of Peter's dresser, became relics of dubious significance. Somewhere in the back of his mind, a cloud was getting bigger.

"Could it be possible that Barbara is keeping company with Lewis?"

That morning Barbara Ross was more important than usual to Peter. Oh yes, he was aware that bigger issues were abroad in the world. Even while Notre Dame and Army had been battling each other that Saturday six months ago, the Polish army was beginning to collapse. Germany was in the field calling signals in the terrible game of war, and men were putting on grimmer helmets in the barracks of England and France than those used by football players. The world was out on one big, complex, combat gridiron.

Yes, even on this very beautiful morning in May, the heavy headlines of the newspapers strewn at Peter's feet were telling about the lightning thrusts and bites of Panzer tanks. All this seemed remote, unrelated, and incomprehensible to Peter. Such physical entities as the Balkans and the Dardanelles were faintly recalled chapters in geography; and Gibraltar was familiar, not because of its strategic position on the world map, but because it was a big rock on the insurance advertisements. Being almost twenty-three years of age, Peter might have been a bit more conscious of his social and civic obligations. He was told that men of twenty-three in other climes and in other countries were well on the way to raising families and conducting themselves with all the poise and responsibility of maturity. More power to them, too. But as for himself, he was merely one American citizen, a slightly overgrown boy in the North Temperate Zone, perfectly satisfied with a life that began early in the morning checking on the regular milking of Holsteins, dreaming of a girl in Massachusetts who might become his wife some day, completely happy with the smell of earth in a ready field and an organ and a piano, on which he loved to play.

But Lewis—this mysterious person who dabbled in din-

The Foundling

ners for two—this Lewis was more portentous of tragedy to him than all the rumblings of far-away battles and the international murmurings of world discontent. Even Hitler himself seemed a minor menace compared to Lewis.

Lewis might steal Barbara's heart between the soup and the demi-tasse.

Yet . . . it was possible Peter might be mistaken.

One night, two weeks later, he discovered that he was not mistaken. It was a quick culmination of events that began with an invitation to attend the wedding of Mark Ross and Elizabeth Kane. The engraved card which respectfully requested the "honor" of his presence was sent by Barbara, and little did she suspect how eagerly he was to jump at so conventional an excuse to come to Lynnford.

Peter went to Lynnford with an electric toaster in his bag and high hope in his heart.

Barbara came slowly down the aisle that morning. She did not know that Peter was in the church. The Nuptial Mass had been celebrated; the organ was playing the Recessional; relatives and friends were smiling and weeping. Mark was a tense but happy groom; the bride was demure. Then Barbara, the bridesmaid! She did not see Peter as she passed.

Later, on the steps of the church where everyone was chattering and laughing, Peter made his way through the crowd.

"Hello, Barbara," he said, stealing up beside her.

"Peter!" She actually shrieked his name and her arms were around him. This was better than anything Peter had hoped for.

"Peter, you came!"

"Sure I came. You sent an invitation."

"But why didn't you write? Why didn't you say you were coming?"

Suddenly the cloud appeared.

"Peter Lane, I believe?" It was Lewis, a chap in his middle twenties, tall, dark, even handsome. He held out his hand. Peter took it.

"Glad to meet you," Peter mumbled. Lewis was resplendent in a cutaway suit, an unusually fancy ascot tie and even a gardenia. Standing beside Barbara, he made a discouragingly dashing figure.

"Lewis was our best man, Peter," Barbara said. Then she introduced Peter to several people whose faces were a gay blur as Lewis escorted her through the maze and the mist of the introductions.

What followed immediately thereafter was not important. Nor was it significant that Peter remained for two extra days in Lynnford at the insistence of Barbara. His old room, within eyeshot of the familiar and ever spinning O. G. Healy, now seemed smaller.

His brief stay in Lynnford might have been a happy one, had it not been for Lewis. For Lewis said something on the evening of the third day, which Peter could not forget.

"I'll take Peter to the station, Barbara," Lewis volunteered that afternoon.

"I'll go, too," Barbara said.

"But there won't be enough room," Lewis answered. "Billy Clayton and Stanley are waiting in the car."

The Foundling

"If it's all the same to you, Lewis, I can take a taxi to the station," Peter said, hoping that Barbara and he could be alone at least for his last moments in Lynnford.

"Think nothing of it, Peter. I'm only too glad to give you a lift."

Shortly afterwards, Peter said good-by to the Ross family. Barbara was waving on the porch when they drove off.

Clayton made the suggestion while the auto was flying over the road. "How about a little drink, Lane?"

"No, thanks."

"Come on. You won't mind a short one," Lewis laughed.

"This is a send-off party, Lane," Clayton added. "A little drink will make your trip to New York painless."

They laughed loudly, and Peter was uncomfortably conscious of being the butt of their "humor." "I just don't drink. However, don't let me spoil your plans."

"You can have a *root*-beer anyway, can't you, Lane?"

Later, they sat over a gleaming black marble table in the tavern.

"What'll it be, Peter?" Lewis asked. "And remember, this is on me."

"I'll have the root-beer Stanley suggested."

Clayton was grinning. "Come on, Lane, order up. You've got privileges in Massachusetts."

"No, thanks." Peter laughed.

About twenty minutes later, Lewis, who was sitting beside Peter, turned and said, "You're all right, Lane. You're not a bad fellow at all."

The Foundling

It was peculiar how chummy one could get over a table in a tavern.

"You're not so bad yourself, Lewis," Peter returned. He was uncomfortable.

"Do you mind if I ask you a personal question, Lane?"

"Go right ahead, Lewis."

"What do you think of Barbara Ross?"

"Why, she's . . . she's a swell girl."

Lewis pursed his lips and jiggled the glass of Scotch in his fingers. "I'm glad you think so, Lane."

Stanley and Clayton were grinning at Peter in complete vacuity. For a moment, he was inclined to play a polite social game of evasions, but the sudden and undeclared challenge in the air could not be dismissed. "Why do you ask, Lewis?"

"What?"

"What you asked about Barbara?"

Lewis laughed deliberately, and he spun the glass in his fingers. "I was merely curious." Then absentmindedly he inspected his class ring.

"Do you mind if I ask you a personal question, Lewis?"

"Not in the least."

"What do *you* think of Barbara Ross?" Peter threw the question back.

"That, my dear boy, is what I would call a leading question," Lewis answered. His gray eyes were looking straight at Peter, and, when Clayton and Stanley laughed, Peter knew that the game was out in the open.

"I don't understand what you mean, Lewis."

"I simply mean that there are certain social details in my life which I won't discuss in public."

"That's a peculiar admission, Lewis."

"You think so?"

"Yes. I'm not afraid to discuss Barbara Ross in public."

"It's not a matter of being *afraid*, Lane."

"You still didn't answer my question."

"What question?"

"I asked you what you think about Barbara Ross."

"And why do you ask?"

"I'm curious, Lewis, just as you were curious a few minutes ago."

Lewis drummed his long fingers on the table. "Would it make much difference to you?"

"It might."

"In what way, Lane?"

"I happen to be interested in Barbara Ross."

Lewis stroked his chin with his fingers like a judge deliberating a pronouncement. "It's too long a time between drinks, fellows."

Clayton and Stanley roared, and Peter felt the blood coming into his face. "Wait a minute, Lewis."

"Yes?"

"You deliberately brought me here to sound me out about Barbara Ross."

"I did?"

"You did. It's as plain as that big gold ring you've got on your finger."

"And what am I supposed to do now, Lane?" His lips were set in straight lines when he faced Peter.

"You still haven't answered my question," Peter smiled. "However, let's skip it."

"No, Lane, we won't skip it." Lewis' fingers were drumming on the table. "Since you're so insistent, Lane, I might tell you this. A girl like Barbara shouldn't be expected to take chances."

"Chances?"

"That's right."

"I don't follow you, Lewis."

He drained his glass and laughed. "A girl like Barbara Ross has a right to expect any person with whom she associates to have a background."

Lewis was completely out in the open now.

"Would you be referring to me?" Peter asked.

"Possibly."

"Would you be referring to my mother and father?"

"Possibly," he said.

The waitress standing near the table screamed when Peter grabbed Lewis and flung him out of the booth. It was done in a sudden blind fury of rage, and if Clayton and Stanley had not leaped between them, the fight would have been an ugly one.

Hours later, Peter sat in the train that rocked southward to New York. The resentment that had burned like a hot fire in his brain was gradually cooling. He knew now that he had put away forever the things of childhood, and that his life was becoming strong and sad with maturity.

He didn't want violence. He hadn't anticipated the bungling, despicable approach of a man whose weakness was becoming more apparent to him as the miles clicked away under the wheels. Lewis was an open book. He was a tall, spoiled, well-groomed boy in love with Barbara. Peter could dismiss Lewis now as easily as snap his fingers.

But there was something more serious than Lewis haunting him that night. In some homes in a smiling, conservative New England town, back there in Massachusetts, families were discussing him, and some of them, sitting under the trees and on the lawns, seemed to be eyeing him in smug respectability and righteousness, saying, "You have no background, Peter."

People were talking about the possibility of an invasion of England that night on the train. The man sitting beside Peter said, "Looks like the Germans will try it any day. They are hammering London to a pulp."

Invasion! Peter was already invaded on a southbound train to New York. He was wide open to all the whispering that goes on behind the drawn curtains in some windows of the little town where lived the girl that Peter hoped to marry.

"Maybe Lewis is right, Barbara," Peter said to himself that night in the train. "Maybe I shouldn't expect you to marry a . . . a question mark like me?" He was a man now, so he did not cry when he said it. He merely breathed it in the half-tones of the pain that was locked in his breast.

The Foundling

Another face then seemed to be looking at him in agony beyond the rattling window of the train. It was the face of his mother as he had dreamed her to have been. And from his heart, he forgave her because he knew somehow she was much younger than he. She was only a slip of a girl crying out of the thunder of a train that went under a tunnel in the night.

Chapter 22

"Don't cut the pieces too small this time," Paul said as he handed Peter the steak. It was the third Tuesday of the month, shortly after Peter's return from Lynnford. They had been making a habit of spending their third Tuesday evenings together in New York. It was their bachelor dinner, as they explained to Ellen, who was not invited and who approved and understood. The simple act of cutting the meat for Paul, who sat patiently with his one arm above the table, was a ceremony Peter would not yield even to the most solicitous of waiters.

Paul had immediately sensed Peter's mood that evening. "What's the matter?" he asked.

"Nothing." Peter was particularly interested in cutting the steak.

"You've got something on your mind."

"Maybe I have," Peter answered with a trace of irritation. It was the first time he had ever spoken that way to Paul.

The Foundling

"Excuse me, Peter. I didn't mean to . . ."

"It's my fault."

Paul took the plate from Peter and the dinner proceeded with half-hearted stabs at conversation. As they left the restaurant, Paul suggested going to a movie.

"Not tonight, Paul. I'd rather not."

"Are you going straight back to Mount Mary?"

"Yes."

They pushed their way slowly through the crowd to the subway. Paul was silent and Peter knew that the night had been a failure.

He faced the thought of walking the long road back to the bungalow that night with no pleasure. It was not the length of the road nor the silence. It was simply the fact of going back to his own thoughts. Life had become confusing and bitter since his return from Lynnford.

Walking down the steps to the subway, Peter studied the side of Paul's face. In a crowd, he appeared always to be solemn. The way he carried his head, the way he walked, the quick turn of his eye to see if Peter was following him—all these were familiar traits Peter had come to know over the years. In that fleeting instant, he realized how much Paul meant to him. He was like some kind silent shadow in all the steps of his life. Overwhelmed with a sense of loneliness in that large crowd, Peter reached out suddenly and caught Paul's arm.

"Wait a minute, Paul. Let's not go home yet."

Paul looked at him in surprise.

"Let's walk, Paul."

The Foundling

"Anything you say."

In the jostling crowd along the street, Peter told him of the incidents and the doubts and fears of the past few days. "It's like a blackness, Paul. I don't know how to express it, except that Lewis kicked the bottom out of things. Maybe I should have expected it. I suppose I always knew it could come up some day . . . some way."

Paul's hand gripped Peter's arm tightly. "It's all right, Peter. Come on. Follow me."

"Where are you going?"

"Just follow me."

Something in the expression of Paul's face discouraged further conversation. They walked rapidly along the street for two blocks and Peter became curious.

"Where are we going, Paul?"

"Never mind. Just keep walking. I want to show you something."

When they rounded Fiftieth Street on Fifth Avenue, he pointed. "You ever see that before?" he asked.

"Certainly. Saint Patrick's Cathedral."

"Just stand here, Peter, and look at it."

The twin spires reared against the dark blue of the night sky. Men and women were walking in and out the doors, and from where they stood the trees on the lawn appeared a bright young green against the stone background of the walls.

Paul's face bore a peculiar, remote expression. "I want you to take a good look at that church."

"I've seen it many times, Paul."

The Foundling

"I guess you have." He smiled then. "Maybe you *have* seen that Cathedral many times. But if you looked at it the way I'm seeing it now, you'd forget every rotten, filthy thing that anyone could say to you or do to you in this life."

Then Paul led Peter as he might have led a child across Fifth Avenue; he led him up the sloping steps and into the Cathedral and then, under the wide and beautiful arches, he pointed out the spot where someone had put him in a manger.

"Right here, Peter. Right *exactly* here is where your mother put you."

He said many things to the boy that night as they stood there. His words, spoken in the hushed tones of a man who was groping with shy and hesitant reverence, coming over Peter's shoulder, as he stood behind him, were the kindest consolation the boy had ever known.

"I wanted to bring you here, Peter," he was saying. "Maybe fifty or sixty times, I've wanted to bring you in here and show you the place where I found you. But you never asked me about it. Not since the day when you were a kid at Mount Mary did you ever mention the subject. So I figured it was best not to say anything more about it. But it's different now. It's something you ought to know, because you're a man. You understand?"

"I understand."

"All right. Listen to me now and remember this as long as you live. Hear me?"

"I hear you."

"Peter, I wasn't fooling that day long ago when I told

you your mother was good. She was human, Peter, and she made a mistake. No one knows the circumstances. But the way I figure it, she did the only thing that a human being who has done wrong can do. She came all the way back to God with her sorrow. And Peter, between me and you, there's no mistake God can't fix up right and proper, Lewis or no Lewis. Understand?"

"I understand."

"And don't forget that."

Mary was beautiful in her Lady Chapel that evening. Even while Paul was speaking, Our Lady of New York seemed to become more beautiful. She seemed to be looking down on the spot where Peter's mother had left him.

Paul stood off to the side when Peter knelt in the Lady Chapel, and because he had brought him out of the shadows of the darkest days he had ever known, Paul, too, was thanked in Peter's earnest, silent prayers.

Twenty minutes later, they were sitting in a little place off Madison Avenue. Paul's scarred face was grave. "Now, here's what you're going to do, Peter."

"Right. What am I going to do?"

"You're going to write that fifth movement . . ."

"Fourth movement, Paul," Peter corrected.

"Fourth movement. You're going to write that fourth movement. Make it your life. Make it as big and important as . . . as the stock and curb exchange business is to these fellows sitting around us."

"Music?"

The Foundling

"Sure. Go out and make a success of it. Go out and prove to all the people like Lewis that you can stand on your own two feet. A girl likes that."

They laughed aloud.

"It's the truth, Peter," Paul continued. "All you need is a little confidence."

Confidence! Peter needed more than confidence in that sprawling world of music. "I can't marry Barbara on music alone, Paul."

"I know you can't. I'm not asking you to marry her on music, any more than I'd ask a woman to marry a fellow on his business prospects. Women don't marry careers. They don't marry architecture, or farming, or medicine. They marry a man, a good solid citizen who can hit a notch in life and keep it. The average girl wants an ideal. She is smart enough to realize that a good grocer is better than a bad president."

Peter laughed and he became more aware of his affection and reverence for Paul.

"And a good musician or whatever you want to call yourself . . ."

"*Composer,* Paul," Peter smiled in mock importance.

"All right. A good composer is as good as a good street cleaner."

Paul was wonderful.

"Write that fourth symphony, Peter, and . . ."

"Fourth movement, Paul."

"All right. Go ahead and write it, and after you've written it, dedicate it to Barbara."

"Maybe Koussevitsky or Toscanini will conduct it," Peter laughed.

"Sure they'll conduct it."

"Maybe I'll be lucky and even the music critics will like it."

"Sure, they'll like it."

"And maybe you and Ellen will be there at Carnegie Hall."

"We'll be there."

"Father Duane and Sister Margaret, too."

"Why not?"

"And Barbara, too?"

"She'll be there, and she'll be proud of you, Peter."

So Peter went back to Mount Mary on a soft cloud. The world, at Paul Taggart's suggestion, was brightening with wide and hopeful horizons of music. Barbara was applauding him and her hands were light cymbals in the air as he fell asleep.

"Wait and see, Barbara," he wrote the next morning. "I'm going to surprise you. I'm working on a Christmas present for you, but I won't tell you what it is now. However, it's something that will come wrapped in strings and I'll deliver it to you personally."

But how was he ever going to finish writing a fourth movement for a symphony? Out in the meadows, that June, when the tedding machine kicked the fresh-cut hay and turned it to the drying warmth of the sun, the fourth movement of a symphony was a comparatively easy thing. When the swallows swept about him in smooth flights catching the insects

The Foundling

he stirred with the knife of the mower, the finale of the symphony was a dream within easy reach. There was exhilaration on the sunny fields of Mount Mary when fragile hopes were built instantly and surely amidst the clatter of farm tools. It was the kind of optimism that had made his music live in the thunder of the subway the night he had left Paul. But it was also the kind of fancy which died in the gray opportunities of silence. For silence, and the clean page, and the poised pen were grim challenges to execution. The chords which throbbed with limitless power and tone in the bright fields, were desiccated and lifeless when Peter sat at the old piano in his bungalow.

It was easy enough to catch the spirit and theme of Sister Crescentia's work, but when he came to the last chord of her andante, he wondered if it ever would be possible for him to fulfill the high standard she had set for the symphony.

Father Duane was understanding when Peter told him about his plans. "Go ahead and finish this symphony, Peter. It shouldn't be too much trouble."

"But it *is* trouble, Father."

"How do you mean?"

"For one thing, I don't know if I'm sufficiently qualified."

"Of course you're qualified. Who said you weren't?"

"That's just my trouble. I have no one to criticize me."

"Criticize you?"

"Yes, Father. I might be barking up the wrong tree."

The old priest wrinkled his nose and surveyed the ceiling. "Do you know Jimmy Gerber?"

The Foundling

"Yes, I've heard of him often."

"Well, you go up to Radio City and tell Jimmy Gerber I sent you. He'll set you straight."

Peter realized again that Father Duane could make things sound awfully simple.

Peter went to Radio City and found the little man sitting behind a desk littered with orchestrations. The reddish moustache that bristled over his mouth was a discouraging distraction, and Peter's first reaction to his bulldoggish stare was an uncomfortable feeling that no man with so fiery an appearance could possibly appreciate the elusive values of music.

"What do you want?" he asked.

"Father Duane told me to see you about a symphony a nun wrote."

"Where is it?"

"It's not completed yet. I'm finishing it for her."

"Well, what do you want to see me for?"

"I wanted to get some advice, sir."

"What kind of advice?"

"I was wondering if I'm qualified to write music, Mr. Gerber."

"That's a very funny question, son," he said. "After twenty years in the business, I'm wondering if *I'm* qualified to *criticize* music."

It was a conversational impasse that called for a cough and explanation. "What I mean is . . . maybe I'm wasting my time."

The Foundling

"Maybe you are, and mine, too," Mr. Gerber agreed crisply.

"How would it be possible to tell, sir?"

"You'd probably have to wait around for sixty years to get that answer."

"Sixty years!"

"Maybe a hundred. Some great composers were not discovered until many years after they died."

A century was an intolerable length of time to wait for approval, Peter thought.

"How long have you been studying music?" Mr. Gerber asked.

"Almost eight years, sir."

"And you want to write symphonic music?"

"Yes sir."

"Where did you study?"

"At Mount Mary under Sister Crescentia."

"Who's Sister Crescentia?"

"She's the Sister who taught music."

"Did you ever go to a conservatory?"

"No sir, I studied privately."

Mr. Gerber's moustache bristled annoyingly. "What's your instrument?"

"Organ and piano."

"How about your orchestration?"

"I have had some instruction, sir."

"What have you studied?"

"I studied Widor and Forsyth."

"That's not enough."

The Foundling

"I've also studied Rimsky-Korsakov."

"That's not enough either. You're only a paper man. Have you enough money to go to a conservatory?"

"No sir."

"Well, how do you expect to write music without an education?"

"I'm not sure, Mr. Gerber. I know I've a long way to go, but I think I have all the orchestration I need right now."

Mr. Gerber shifted on his swivel chair and laughed. "So you think you have all the orchestration you need?"

"Yes sir."

"How would you know?" He was still laughing.

"I learned the alto and treble clefs in four months, Mr. Gerber."

"That's not unusual."

"I've also followed the best music ever recorded with conductor score sheets."

Mr. Gerber twisted his moustache meditatively. "Why did you do that?"

"Because I loved music and wanted to understand every value of instrument mixture I could learn."

"Instrument mixture?"

"Combinations, sir."

The sharp eyes studied Peter closely. "Have you ever written anything?"

"Short pieces for trios and quartettes."

"And what about your composition?"

"I don't understand what you mean, Mr. Gerber."

The Foundling

"Do you think it's good? Did anybody ever tell you it was good? What was the criticism?"

"I never submitted anything I've written to anyone but nuns."

Mr. Gerber rose from his chair and went to the window. The silver dolphin paper-weights that lay on top of his high stack of correspondence were glistening in the sunlight that came through the window. It made for an extremely frigid and metallic atmosphere and Peter was tempted to make as quick an exit as diplomacy and good taste would allow.

"I've got a peculiar theory about music, son," Mr. Gerber said, still looking out the window. "You can take it for what it's worth." He faced Peter and tamped a cigarette on the nail of his thumb. "Music is not a mechanical business, despite all you learn from the professors and the books. Music is as mad, beautiful, and instantaneous as the thought and mood that inspire it."

And then he flung the challenge. "In other words, a man is making a mistake if he can't make music fall from his fingers at, I won't say a moment's notice, but a *second's* notice."

"A second's notice?"

"A split-second's notice, the time equivalent that it takes inspiration to send rage or pity into the voice of a man."

Mr. Gerber's rough, ugly moustache bristled in the sun; but a spark of kinship leaped between Peter and this small, volcanic creature at that moment.

"I don't claim to be the world's greatest authority on music," he added. "But I can tell you this. Unlike literature,

The Foundling

unlike poetry, unlike any of the arts, music comes in quick flashes. A poet can trim his lines, a sculptor can mould, and chisel, but music's got to come like the breaths of spirits. It's got to be inspired."

This was still in the high realms of theory and Peter began to have passing doubts about Sister Crescentia's work. "It comes instantaneously, Mr. Gerber?"

"Right."

"But this nun took almost five years to write three movements."

Mr. Gerber laughed loudly. "Sure. It might take you ten years to write three bars. But when you write those bars, they've got to come like a flash of light. It might take fifty years to write a symphony; but it takes only a matter of seconds to think and feel the music of that symphony. That's why you've got so many musicians who are not successful. They can't write fast enough for their inspiration when they've got it, and they can't wait long enough for inspiration when they haven't got it.

"Take it from me, son," Mr. Gerber went on, "you can make a living a lot easier in a building trade or a factory. We've got hundreds of Beethovens, Chopins and Bachs floating around New York right now. I mean it. But most of them will wind up in a Greenwich Village flat with a baloney sandwich and anemia but they live with the music they love and would choose no other life."

"But I *want* to write music, Mr. Gerber. More than anything else in the world, I want to write music. And I believe in Sister Crescentia."

The Foundling

Mr. Gerber smiled condescendingly like a man who has long been exposed to the familiar but futile dreams of artists.

"You came here to find out if you were qualified to write music."

"Yes, sir."

"That's the first request of the kind I've ever received. They usually turn up in this office with a half dozen symphonies under their arms." He opened a door at the rear of the office and peered into a room. "Tell you what I'll do as long as you're curious. Would you mind stepping into this room?"

It was a bare room—bare save for a piano, a majestic grand, standing austerely under the barred light that filtered through the Venetian blinds.

"Sit down, son."

Peter sat on the piano stool and wondered what was to come next.

"All right, son. Now I want you to think. Think about some music you've heard."

"What kind of music?"

"Any music."

It was an odd bit of business. Owing either to the overwhelming presence of Mr. Gerber, or to a simple state of nerves, or both, Peter could not recall a single phrase of music.

Mr. Gerber waited for a few minutes and then he asked, "What have you in mind?"

"I'm afraid, Mr. Gerber, I don't quite follow you."

The Foundling

The brusque critic sat in a chair near the piano and fixed his sharp eyes on the boy. "Do you know anything from Haydn?"

"Not too much."

"Sibelius?"

"Oh, yes sir."

"Mmmmm . . . let's see. You know the *Swan of Tuonela*?"

"Yes sir."

"How would you describe it?"

"Mournful."

"Certainly it's mournful. But what else?"

"Well, Sibelius described his English horn as gliding over a black river. But I've always felt that the horn wasn't gliding."

"No?"

"No. It seems to be flying instead."

"Flying?" Mr. Gerber was smiling.

"Flying, yes sir. Flying straight to death."

"Why do you say that?"

"The horn is a bit high and it tumbles in a kind of flight, sir. However, I've never seen a swan fly."

"I've never seen one fly either," Mr. Gerber laughed. "But I know what you mean."

"Sibelius also has a lot of water that cascades in the opening passages, and it's not the black river he said it was."

Mr. Gerber was still smiling.

"In fact, I think it runs a bit like a waterfall."

The narrow room rang with Mr. Gerber's laughing. And

then he made a most encouraging remark. "I think, perhaps, you might know how to write music, son."

"Thank you, Mr. Gerber."

"All right. Play me another *Swan of Tuonela*."

"A variation, you mean?"

"That's right. Something with the gloom and misery of life."

Peter sat at the piano, frowning.

"I want only a few bars, twenty or thirty at the most. And you can take all the time you want, son."

Sister Crescentia's dark key of C minor came to his mind, and he started. The instrument was superbly sensitive, unbelievably, almost ridiculously, unlike the long-battered relic in the bungalow at the Mount.

For two or three minutes, Peter searched the minors in the low register, trying to catch the theme Mr. Gerber had suggested. This direct invitation to improvise on a given subject was the kind of challenge he had often imagined. But the atmosphere in a room of bright chrome and green leather, the almost over-sensitive key action of the piano, and the awareness of Mr. Gerber sitting at his side watching him, were almost unbearably oppressive.

"Take your time, son," Mr. Gerber said quietly.

Then Peter drew the invisible curtain around him slowly as Theresa Bordano the blind girl had done years ago in Mount Mary. It was as if the sunlight went out of the room, the leather and chrome dissolved, and he was standing again in a misty night, looking back at candles gleaming through drawn shutters. Almost imperceptibly, the music stole upon him, the utter sadness of the Gregorian requiem, Sister Crescentia's requiem, and into this he wove the variations of his own life—the faces of men and women he had seen in the newspapers, tortured with the daily tragedies of life.

When Peter stopped playing, Mr. Gerber was twisting his moustache and staring at the floor.

"That's not so good, Mr. Gerber. Perhaps, if I had more time to think about . . ."

"That's splendid, son. That's actually splendid."

Five minutes later, Peter walked quickly along the gleaming floors of the RCA Building. These people down here, these hurrying busy hundreds of people, these elevator men, messenger girls, harassed executives, these casual out-of-town visitors standing in groups below the somber giants sprawling on the murals, all these people down here did not know that he, Peter Lane, had just completed an engagement with Mr. James L. Gerber. They did not know that he had actually sat at Mr. Gerber's piano. Nor did they know how enthusiastic Mr. Gerber had been when he heard Peter's improvisation.

"That's splendid, son. That's actually splendid," Mr. Gerber had said.

Peter stepped out into the sunny streets of midtown Manhattan, secretly amused at the millions of people who were as yet unaware that a potential composer was walking in their midst.

Chapter 23

MR. GERBER'S approval sent Peter headlong into the mysteries of composition, and he attacked the business of the fourth movement with all the gusto of a Berlioz. In the quiet of the night when Mount Mary was asleep, he went to his piano in the bungalow, and after carefully drawing the shades lest any tell-tale light reveal to the Sisters what late hours he was keeping, he continued on his symphonic ways. The clandestine atmosphere even added to his stature as an artist, Peter thought. Masterpieces were usually violent and beauteous products of storm and strife, created not in ease but discomfort. Masterpieces had to be worked and sweated for. Did not Bach himself have to contend with the tonal imperfections of the instruments of his day? Did not Abraham Lincoln write a world-stirring address on the back of an old envelope? Perhaps centuries from now some biographer would allude to the fact that Peter Lane, American heir of

Finland's Sibelius, had to compose at two o'clock in the morning on a rickety old piano in an old bungalow.

"How's it coming?" Paul Taggart invariably asked that summer.

"I'll have it finished by September, Paul," Peter would invariably guarantee.

One night, when he was deep in a sweep of trumpets, Father Duane knocked and entered the bungalow. The old priest consulted his watch deliberately in the doorway.

"Do you know what time it is, Peter?"

"About one o'clock, Father."

"It's one thirty. One thirty in the morning. You can't follow this schedule night after night and continue with the work you're doing on the property."

"I don't mind staying up, Father."

"But you can't do it. It will wear you out. Why do you have to stay up so late?"

"I haven't enough time to work at the piano."

Father Duane thrust his fingers through his white hair. "Well, you just can't continue like this, Peter," he insisted. "You'll have to make some other arrangements. Now get to bed like a good man."

"All right, Father."

"And maybe you'd better take a sleep-over."

"Jim's expecting me to report to him in the early morning."

"Never mind Jim. I'll take care of him. Get enough sleep. The cows and pianos will be here long after you're dead and gone."

"Yes, Father."

Peter was embarrassed to think that he had disturbed the old priest. In the bungalow, the memory of Father Duane's tousled head in the doorway disconcertingly intruded upon the glorious trumpet passage he had just begun to compose.

The dream continued.

Sitting in the iron saddle of the tractor, with the double-disc harrow set at Jim Randall's strict "three inches, mind you, and not a shave deeper," Peter jounced through the vegetable plants with a pad on his knee and a fortissimo in his head. He paused in the shade of the maple trees, and the engine sent a mighty obbligato to the hurried notes he scribbled across the sheet. This scrawl across the pad was but the germ of a musical phrase, a mere kernel for growth and later cultivation.

Music spoke to him in all the random movements of the day. There was music in the spray of nicotine sulphate shot on the copper beeches and the dogwood, music in the tremolo of the pumps that blew the green hay and molasses into the tall silos. Whether he walked through the tumbling tomato plants, or fingered the glass frames for moisture in the south field; whether he mixed the bran and bone meal for the yearling heifers, or stood with an authoritative pencil over the dairy books making notations on milk yield and fat tests; he was never long without humming flashes of what was to be, undoubtedly, the worthy finale of Sister Crescentia's symphony.

"Have you nearly finished it?" Paul continued to ask.

"I'll finish it soon," Peter calculated.

The Foundling

"September?"

"Well, maybe November."

"You'd better hurry up if you want to make it a Christmas present for Barbara."

"I'll surely have it completed by December, Paul. I'm certain of it. It'll be ready for Barbara, all wrapped in strings."

But Peter's calculations were wide and wrong. The long hours spent at transposing the pencil notes to the separate orchestral scores, occasional deep plunges into shadows of doubt, the changes he made necessitating the copying and the recopying of entire pages, the laborious process of condensing the work for the conductor's score, and, worst of all, the discouraging decisions to perfect or eliminate faulty passages and sometimes make bad matters worse—all this consumed more time than he had anticipated.

"Barbara, please excuse all the false alarms," Peter wrote that December. "I wanted to be there with you this Christmas with the present I promised. Remember? The one I told you would come all wrapped in strings? Of course, I'm sending you a present anyway 'in strings.' But it's not what I planned on. Sooner than you expect, however, I'll bring you something else. And I'm sure you're going to like it."

It was difficult to conceal his enthusiasm whenever he wrote to Barbara in veiled allusions to the symphony. Many times, that winter, he thought how proud Barbara would be of him when he became a success.

Then came June.

The last note had been written; the ink had dried; the finale was complete.

The Foundling

"It took you a long, long time," Paul said that afternoon on the upper deck of the Fifth Avenue bus. "But I guess it was worth it."

"I hope so, Paul."

The precious thick envelope lying on his knee filled Peter with high promise.

"What are you going to do now, Peter?"

"I'm going to leave it with Mr. Gerber at Radio City."

"That's right. I'd forgotten Father Duane had sent you to him. If there's anyone in New York who can give you the boost you need, it's Gerber," Paul said.

"I'm not really looking for a boost."

"No?"

"No. I think this music will stand on its own merit. Honestly, I do, Paul."

Paul stared straight ahead.

"At least I hope it stands on its merits," Peter added, growing less certain of himself as the bus got closer and closer to Radio City.

The New York Public Library was white and friendly in the sun when they passed Forty-second Street. The library was, in a way, the *alma mater* to much that was now wrapped in Peter's envelope. He recalled Mr. Hopper, the kindly helpful director. He remembered the long afternoons spent in the music section, the golden hours devoted to dreaming the dreams of Bach, Beethoven, and Brahms. He remembered the reverence with which he used to walk into the small music room with the long table in the middle and the music lovers, some in their 'teens, some in their seventies, studying the scores. One he remembered particularly, an old man dressed in speckled gray with black braid trimming the lapels of his jacket; he always called for Richard Strauss and, as he read, he used to lead an imaginary orchestra with his pencil. Would anyone, Peter used to wonder, ever ask for the Lane compositions? Would Peter Lane ever join that select, jealous group of the music immortals?

But, on the upper deck of the bus that day, he was not dreaming of immortality. "Just to have *her* listen to me once! Just to have Barbara sit beside me when the orchestra is tuning up! To see her face grow excited and proud when the roof of Carnegie Hall is ringing with the brass and woodwinds," he thought. "If I could have her for one minute like that, listening to the music I wrote, it would be worth it all."

The girl who sat at the desk outside Mr. Gerber's office was pretty and precise.

"Your name, sir?"

"Peter Lane."

"Have you an appointment with Mr. Gerber?"

"No, I haven't."

"Would you mind taking a seat over there, please?"

The girl talked on the phone for a few seconds, and then informed him that Mr. Gerber was being detained at an important executive meeting. Was there anything she could do?

"Well, I've got music here which I want Mr. Gerber to see."

"You may leave it with me, sir. I'll see that he gets it."

"Perhaps I'd better come back tomorrow."

"Mr. Gerber is a very busy man, sir."

The Foundling

Peter surrendered the envelope to the young lady reluctantly. "You're sure Mr. Gerber will get this music?"

"Yes sir."

As Paul and he walked along the street later, Peter's worries began to grow.

"That girl may forget my music, Paul, especially during lunch hour." Peter had a harrowing vision of his envelope being absently stuffed into a drawer with a detective story or even into the waste paper basket with a half-eaten lettuce and tomato sandwich. "What would I do if she ever lost that music?"

"Stop worrying about that music, Peter. Is it to the Rainbow room or Schrafft's that we'll go?"

"Maybe Gerber *was* really having a board meeting, Paul."

"Of *course* he was having a board meeting, Peter. Quit worrying about it. He'll probably give you a ring on the phone in the morning."

Indeed! That's exactly what Mr. Gerber would do. He'd call in the morning and his voice would be excited, enthusiastic. "One of the greatest pieces of music I have ever examined, Lane!" That's what Mr. Gerber would say.

"Sure he will; let's go to a quiet corner in the Biltmore, Paul."

Over the luncheon, Peter suddenly became serious.

"Paul?"

"Yes?"

"That music's just got to be good."

"What's bothering you now?"

The Foundling

"I'm thinking about my . . . well, my future, Paul."

"You've got your future already cut out for you."

"Maybe." Peter's eyes brightened slowly. "If that music's accepted and published, I . . . I could ask Barbara Ross to marry me."

"Sure."

"There's pretty good money in music, isn't there, Paul?"

"Yes, if one makes good, Peter, and I am sure you will."

"If I can only make a name for myself, it'll be a cinch. That's the way it works, Paul. A few good contracts! Maybe a steady job right here in Radio City!" Peter was ensnared by his favorite vision. "I wouldn't be ashamed to ask Barbara to marry me on that."

Taggart laughed. "And best of all, Peter, it's already June."

Yes, it was June.

Most fortunately and coincidentally, it was June.

Peter dreamed all the way back in the ferry that evening. The symphony would be approved in June, purchased in June, contracted for in June; and in less than three weeks, he'd be off to Lynnford with a professionally printed version of the work under his arm. In June, when the world is young and green, he could go to Massachusetts. And in June, perhaps . . . "In June, I'll ask Barbara Ross to marry me!"

Now, if only Mr. Gerber would cooperate.

Peter waited hopefully the next morning for the telephone call. Two days, three days, a week. No word from Mr. Gerber. Several phone calls to his office brought the same reply. "Mr. Gerber is not available at present, sir. Any message?"

The Foundling

On the Tuesday of the third week in June, the truck that carried the mail to Mount Mary stopped outside his door.

"Peter Lane?" the driver asked.

"Yes."

"Special delivery."

Peter recognized the envelope, even before the driver stepped from the truck. Tearing it open in a fever of expectation, he found a white sheet of engraved paper pinned to the music. It was terse, emphatic, official.

"The first three movements are unusual, even magnificent at times [Sister Crescentia had passed the test], but the fourth or finale movement, lacks something. In the opinion of Doctor Sperti, it becomes ineffective, meaningless, and at times puerile. These also are my own unbiased sentiments. A drastic revision is necessary I feel. With all good wishes . . ."

With all good wishes, he remained, sincerely, James L. Gerber.

Ineffective! Meaningless! Puerile! With three lethal adjectives, these critics had passed judgment on many months, in fact many years, of work. Peter walked to Jim Randall's cottage in a stupor.

"I won't be in to help you tonight, Jim."

"All right, Peter."

He had to be out somewhere on a road, walking, moving. He had to get away from the neat, burning stigma that was written across a page in elite type. To get away from the criticism of people, this was what he wanted.

He rested that morning somewhere along a beach. The water was falling in small waves against the shore.

The Foundling

It was not only despair that hung heavily on him. It was also the utter depression that followed the revelation of his own inadequacy.

He poked the sand with a dry, bleached stick. "This is how it's always been," he thought. "Just poking at things. Never doing anything really right. Why, I'm not even a good farmer. Not even a good milker. I was never able to beat Jim at the pails. I can't even turn a harrow without piling the dirt at the top of the row."

All the inadequacies of his life were suddenly magnified by those three typewritten words—ineffective, meaningless, puerile. "Why, I can't even hit a nail straight without leaving half dollars in the wood."

One criticism did all this to him. And, thinking of Gerber's letter lying ominously on his dresser back at the bungalow, Peter knew that Barbara was painfully out of reach. Barbara could never marry someone who was ineffective, meaningless and puerile.

June and Barbara were fading fast, and when Peter Lane looked at his hands, he began to tremble in loneliness and defeat.

Paul Taggart breathed heavily over the table in the restaurant that night. "All right. Suppose you *didn't* write a good fourth symphony . . ."

"Fourth movement, Paul."

"Whatever you call it. Suppose you didn't. Is that any reason why you can't go up to Lynnford and see Barbara?"

"I promised her a big surprise."

The Foundling

"Surprise!" Taggart snorted. "Listen. You go to Lynnford and that'll be surprise enough for her."

"Wait a minute, Paul." Peter sipped a glass of water slowly. "I can't fool myself any longer. I've been living in a fool's paradise for years. But it's over now."

"You've got no backbone. That's the trouble with you, Peter."

"It isn't that. It's simply trying to figure myself out . . . trying to know what I can do with my life."

"But you're young yet."

"Sure. Young enough to think I could make my bread and butter with music. Young enough to think I could ask Barbara to marry me on a piece of orchestration. Well, I woke up this afternoon."

Taggart gestured impatiently. "All right, then. What are you going to do with yourself?"

"I don't know yet. I'm dizzy trying to think."

Paul ran his fingers through his hair in vexation. "Listen, if it's money you need . . ."

"No, thanks, Paul."

"But I *want* you to continue with your music, Peter. Maybe if you were to get some more studying in a conservatory . . ."

"Thanks just the same. I appreciate it. I really do. But I'm through living off other people. I've got to get out on my own."

"Isn't there anything I can do?"

"Sure." Peter was trying hard to smile. "Find me a job with a big future."

The Foundling

"A job? You mean you're leaving Mount Mary, too?"

"That's right."

"Where are you going to get a job these days?"

"That's what I'm trying to find out myself."

Taggart shook his head in desperation. "You're making a big mistake, Peter. If you deliberately give up all your music . . ."

"Don't mention music now. Please, Paul." Peter's face was white and strained. "Do you think for a minute I *want* to give it up. I don't. Some of the happiest hours of my life were with that old organ back there at the Mount. Why, I . . ." Peter was faltering, "I built some swell dreams on that music . . . dreams for Barbara and me. But that's all they were, Paul. Nothing but dreams."

"Yeah." Paul was weary. "I understand."

"So now I start from scratch."

"Okay, Peter. Okay. But where are you going to get this job?"

"I don't know. Just give me time."

Taggart was still troubled.

Peter sipped the water and stared directly into Paul's eyes. "Speaking of time, Paul, how long will a girl wait for you?"

"Barbara?"

"Yes."

"Oh . . . anywhere from five minutes to . . . to eternity."

Peter smiled. "You're a real friend, Paul."

Chapter 24

THE FOLLOWING day was a blue one. It was especially blue for Snoggins Mulrooney. The old sacristan was in an aggressive mood. He was sweeping the steps of the church, and heaping, at the same time, imprecations upon the heads of all the young heathens who persisted in showering bridal couples with rice. "I hate rice," he muttered. "I despise and detest rice," he grumbled. If Snoggins had his way, he would have petitioned the Holy Father himself to pronounce immediate and everlasting excommunication upon anybody who was caught within a half mile of a wedding with a "drop of rice on him."

Just then, as if Providence were bent upon trying him to the utmost, Miss Louise Benburston, the organist of St. Rita's, stepped daintily down the steps over the rice. The tall, owlish-looking lady, forever in possession of a canvas briefcase

The Foundling

crammed with copies of church music, said sweetly, "It was a beautiful wedding, wasn't it, Mr. Mulrooney?"

Snoggins growled after her as she headed toward the rectory.

At that moment, Paul Taggart stopped near the church steps. "Good evening, Mr. Mulrooney."

"How do you do?" Snoggins said, making a savage swipe with his broom.

"You're looking well, Mr. Mulrooney."

Snoggins growled again. "Faith, and it's a miracle I'm alive. If we have any more rice-weddin's around here, I'll resign. I've swept ten tons of rice off the steps of St. Rita's if I've swept an ounce." He shook the broom for emphasis. "As if I had nothing more to do than be jibbin' and jabbin' with a broom on the steps of a church, when I should be," Snoggins forced a sepulchral cough, "when I should be home in my sick-bed."

Paul sympathized with the aging sacristan.

Later, the conversation swung towards Peter Lane.

"And how is the boy?"

"Oh, not so good these days," Paul answered.

"What's the trouble with him?"

"He's down in his boots."

"That's so?" Snoggins was getting interested. "Anything I can do to help?"

"I came over here purposely to see you, Mr. Mulrooney. I believe you can give me some advice."

Snoggins took a deep, pleased breath. "Shoot! What can I do for you?"

Paul told Snoggins about Peter's decision to give up music. "You see, he thinks he's wasting his time. He wants to leave Mount Mary and get a job."

"I see."

"I was thinking, if he could get a job as organist in some church, it would be a great help and it would be the right kind of work for him. In other words, Mr. Mulrooney, I believe Peter's cut out for music . . . some kind of music."

"I see."

"How would you suggest going about it?"

Snoggins extracted his snuff box and proceeded to paint a discouraging picture of organists in the abstract and in the flesh. "It's a most peculiar kind of job, and they're most peculiar kind of people, Mr. Taggart." Snoggins was thinking particularly of Miss Louise Benburston, that ever-pressing thorn in his side. He had accused her several times lately with deliberately choosing the slowest and longest selections for the choir. That was a sad state of affairs, indeed, since it had frequently interfered with the prompt schedules of the Masses, leaving the ten o'clock congregation bumping into the eleven o'clock congregation and, to put it in a nutshell, gumming up the works generally. "Yes sir, they're most peculiar kind of people. Organists live for years, and years, and years, and they remain organists up to the last day of their lives."

"Then you don't think Peter could find a job as an organist anywhere in New York, Mr. Mulrooney?"

"Well now, I didn't say that," Snoggins corrected. "I

The Foundling

merely said that I can't think of anything rarer than an organist who wants to quit."

"I see."

"I'm sorry, Mr. Taggart. I don't think I can help . . ." Snoggins stopped abruptly. He removed his derby and started to fan himself. "Wait a minute."

"What is it, Mr. Mulrooney?"

"Wait a minute. Let me think." The gleam in Mulrooney's eyes was growing more intense.

While Paul waited there outside the church, Snoggins' thoughts were skipping quickly back over the years. His memory was running to a side street in upper Manhattan to a dry-goods store on 125th Street. It was all so very long ago.

"Let me think for a minute, Mr. Taggart."

Snoggins remembered it all clearly now: the pretzel wagon at the corner, the stand where the man sold fruit, the Italian who sold the reddest tomatoes. But he remembered especially the dry-goods store. The dry-goods store of long ago.

"Just give me a minute to think, Mr. Taggart."

The pictures flashed in lightning procession across Snoggins Mulrooney's mind. There was a piano playing in the rear of the dry-goods store. A young boy was playing the piano in slow, laborious scales. Yes, it was clear again. Irwin Hecht, proprietor, was standing behind the counter once more.

"Let me think for a minute, Mr. Taggart."

Snoggins Mulrooney was a boy again. He was standing on the threshold of a dry-goods store. He was asking for a pair

The Foundling

of Drummer Boy stockings. He was reaching for a quarter. He was suddenly embarrassed, frightened, ashamed. He was telling Irwin Hecht, proprietor, he lost the quarter. He was very young. He was almost crying. A whole quarter. And Mr. Irwin Hecht smiled slowly, patiently, and wrapped the Drummer Boy stockings in crinkly paper.

"Let me think for just a minute, Mr. Taggart."

Yes, the pictures were getting clearer. Snoggins Mulrooney was a young boy with deep admiration for a man who wrapped a pair of Drummer Boy stockings in crinkly paper. For free. For nothing. He was getting more friendly with Mr. Hecht. He remembered Mr. Hecht when he called him into the back room; when he showed him the piano; when he introduced him to his fourteen-year-old son, Gabriel; when he told him he would spend his life's blood on his son, Gabriel. Gabriel, who loved music!

"Let me think for just a moment, Mr. Taggart."

Coming back, now, in sharper focus was that day in October. Willie Mulrooney, in Drummer Boy stockings, was walking through the marketplace in October, walking through the odors of roasting chestnuts, dill pickles and pumpernickel, walking again through the haggling, and poverty, and penny-pinching bargain battles in October. He was seeing, again, Irwin Hecht, proprietor, sitting in a chair, sobbing and twisting muslin in his fingers. And he was asking Irwin Hecht, store-keeper, what was the matter? And Irwin Hecht was muttering something in Yiddish, something Willie Mulrooney couldn't understand.

"What's the trouble, Mr. Hecht?"

The Foundling

"Gabe. Gabe is sick."

"Yeah?"

"He's bad."

"Yeah?"

"My son. My little boy," the man sobbed.

"Don't worry, Mr. Hecht. Gabe will be all right."

"No, Willie. He's going to die on me." Mr. Hecht looked mournfully into the streets.

"Why don't you put him into a hospital, if he's going to die?" Willie Mulrooney asked.

"Hospital?" Irwin Hecht gestured helplessly. "I haven't got a cent."

"No money?"

Mr. Hecht waved his arm over the counters of hair ribbons, smocks, drapes. "This bankrupts me."

That statement was in line with some of the whisperings of the fellows on the corner. "Fire Sales." "Bankruptcy." "Selling Out." But Willie Mulrooney wondered for a minute. He paused. He thought of the bearded, hungry-looking men in his own neighborhood who searched the ash cans for rags and cardboard. Willie Mulrooney was puzzled.

"You mean you really haven't got any money, Mr. Hecht?"

"I haven't got twenty dollars."

"Yeah?"

"And Gabe is dying."

"What's the matter with Gabe?"

"Cancer."

Cancer! Young Willie Mulrooney shuddered. He had

known cancer. He sat in a room with his own mother and had seen her dying with cancer. He had seen her grow ashen gray, weak with cancer. He had sat with his mother and lifted her in his young arms as he might have lifted a child. He, Willie Mulrooney, had seen the ravages and the pain that can come across the body of someone you love.

"Cancer, Mr. Hecht?"

"He's going to die. My boy, Gabriel, is going to die." Mr. Hecht was inconsolable.

"Hold on a second, Mr. Hecht. Just a second, please."

William Snoggins Mulrooney, for this brief instant, was living again in a far October. He was running madly through the marketplace again, through the crowds, through all the loud, huckstering noises of life. And he was knocking at a door again. And a nun with a black bonnet answered his knock. And the explanations were made. And an old nun nodded, and sighed, and said, "All right, boy. All right. We'll be there."

Gabriel Hecht, son of Irwin Hecht, died in the arms of a nursing nun twenty-four miles out of New York. The house he died in bore a simple inscription: Rose Hawthorne Home for Cancerous Poor. And when Irwin Hecht walked away from the gray building that day with Willie Mulrooney, he cried beside a hawthorn hedge.

"Willie," he said, "Willie. My boy died in peace and in as little pain as possible. He, a young Jewish boy whose father was broke . . . those Catholic women took him in like he was their very own and cared for him. That has taught me something, Willie. That is the lesson that Gabe's going

The Foundling

has taught me. Those nuns don't close doors; anybody can come in for help. That's the way I will live now, Willie, for Gabe and for those nuns. No closed doors. That's the way everybody in the world should live." That was what Irwin Hecht said to Willie Mulrooney by the hawthorn bush outside the Home for Cancerous Poor.

"Let me think, Mr. Taggart," repeated Snoggins Mulrooney.

Paul Taggart shifted uncomfortably outside St. Rita's Church.

"Did you ever hear of Ike Hecht?" Snoggins suddenly asked.

"Ike Hecht?"

"Irwin Hecht."

"Oh, you mean the fellow who owns . . . ?"

"The fellow who owns Hecht's Department Store. Ike Hecht and I are just like that!" Snoggins snapped his fingers impressively.

"What about him?"

"I think Ike can help us, Mr. Taggart."

"You mean Hecht can get Peter a job as an organist?"

"I ain't saying a thing. I just got an idea." Then William Snoggins Mulrooney waved his broom like a scepter and declared, "And when Mulrooney gets an idea, *Mulrooney gets an idea*!"

Three quarters of an hour later, a somber-faced butler ushered a wheezing sacristan and a one-armed man into the plush home of Irwin Hecht.

The Foundling

"Ike's doing all right, ain't he?" Snoggins remarked in a loud aside that lifted the butler's eyebrow.

"Mr. Hecht will see you in the library," the butler said. "This way, gentlemen."

"Some class, eh, Mr. Taggart?" Snoggins observed as he settled into a soft chair.

"Beautiful house, all right."

"Ike was always dut-dut."

Paul smiled at Mulrooney's "dut-dut," which was accompanied by a flutter of fat fingers signifying taste, class, distinction, elegance, and several other social graces, too complicated and numerous to be defined by mere language.

"Willie!"

"Ike!"

The aged Mr. Hecht strode across the room and flung his arms around the fat sacristan. "Willie, you're a sight for old eyes. Where have you been? What've you been doing?"

The following few minutes turned out to be a series of expostulations, congratulations, and back-slapping so vigorous that it set both men to coughing.

"You're getting old, Willie," Hecht, the octogenarian, remarked.

"Not so's you can see it." Snoggins proudly displayed a thatch of graying hair as against the bald and sterile expanse of Mr. Hecht's head. "That's the trouble with you fellows, Ike. You start making money and you lose hair."

Irwin Hecht laughed, and for the first time he noticed Paul Taggart. "Excuse me, sir. I didn't mean to be rude."

"Shut up, Ike," Snoggins interrupted. "Stop pretending to be the gentleman. You were the cutest dry-goods salesman around 125th Street."

"And you were the toughest customer east of Second Avenue."

"Your Drummer Boy stockings were plain robbery."

"Twenty-five cents, Willie. A bargain."

"A bargain? They left welts in my toes and blisters on my heel the size of a duck egg."

Hecht doubled with laughter. "It was your winter underwear, Willie. You can't put Drummer Boy stockings over winter underwear."

"Faith, and I did put stockings over my winter underwear. My mother showed me how. Where else could you put stockings?"

"You're asking me?" Hecht was in a spasm of hysteria. "That winter underwear! Everytime you came into the store, I thought your legs were going to explode, Willie."

Snoggins rippled slowly into a roar and the library rang with the laughter of old memories.

When the room settled to quietness, Snoggins broached the subject. "Ike, I'd like you to do me a favor."

"Certainly."

"This Mr. Taggart has a boy, an orphan boy who's interested in music."

"So?"

"He needs a good job and a . . . well, he needs to have some help to complete his musical education."

"So?"

The Foundling

Paul interrupted, and quickly and nervously outlined the story of Peter Lane.

"You know this boy well, Mr. Taggart?" the aged Hecht asked.

"Just as if he were my own son," Paul answered.

"I see." Mr. Hecht drummed his fingers on the arm of his chair. "He likes music, Mr. Taggart?"

"Yes, sir. I think music is . . . I think Peter Lane's made for music, Mr. Hecht."

"So?"

Snoggins shifted in his chair. "Ike, I wouldn't be troubling you with this if I didn't remember what you said to me six years ago."

"I said something to you six years ago?"

"Indeed you did. I met you outside . . ."

"Sure, I remember, Willie," Mr. Hecht interrupted. "I remember. It was outside my store."

"That's right, Ike."

"I said to you . . ." Mr. Hecht's eyes closed in memory of the day. "I said to you, 'Willie, I'm a successful man. I got one of the biggest stores in New York. But I can't forget the other days. The people I knew. People like you. So, I owe you one good favor in life. One good favor for Gabe.'"

"That's what you said, Ike. Exactly!" Snoggins affirmed. "One good favor for Gabe."

"I appreciate what you did for my son, Gabriel, Willie."

"Aw, it was nothing."

"No. It was everything. I didn't have a penny those days. I was broke."

"Those nuns did it."

"Yes, I know, Willie. I'll never forget."

"So," Mr. Hecht continued after a moment, "so what do you want me to do?"

Snoggins pointed to Paul. "Tell him, Mr. Taggart."

Paul's lips were dry. It was the first time he had ever made an appeal for any man's favor. "I think this boy deserves a good musical education, Mr. Hecht."

"So?"

"And he hasn't the money. He hasn't a job with . . . well, the kind of job that will allow him the time for his music."

"So? He doesn't have a job. What else?"

"Well, it's this way . . ." Paul floundered.

But Snoggins came to Paul's rescue. "Ike, to put it in a nutshell, could you set up the kid?"

Mr. Hecht smiled at the directness of the fat sacristan's question. "Set him up, Willie?"

"Yeah, Ike. Set him up right."

"Come here," Mr. Hecht invited. "Over here. Follow me. I want to show you something."

The three men entered a room that was brilliant with flowers, silver pieces, antiques, and potteries.

"Look, Willie. Over there on the wall." Mr. Hecht indicated the picture.

It was an enlarged photograph, colored by hand, of fourteen-year-old Gabriel Hecht.

"That's my son, Mr. Taggart."

"Beautiful picture, Mr. Hecht," Paul said.

The Foundling

"The best boy who ever lived, Gabe was." Then the man walked to a piano that was set directly beneath the picture. "And this piano . . . fifteen years ago I bought it. In memory of Gabriel I bought it. He always wanted to play piano."

Snoggins smiled. "That's why I came here tonight, Ike. I remembered the old piano on 125th Street."

"Gabe would have liked this one," Hecht continued proudly. "Look at it. Special case. Concert grand. Walnut." Irwin Hecht tapped the piano with his knuckles. "In memory of Gabriel, I bought it." A shadow of pain passed over the face of the old man, as he stood there looking up at the picture, and then his voice broke slightly. "In memory of Gabriel who loved music."

Snoggins bent his head and genuine tears were rolling down his face.

"All right, Mr. Taggart," Hecht said. "Tell your boy to come and see me tomorrow."

"Thanks, Mr. Hecht," Paul breathed.

"Thanks, Ike," Snoggins boomed.

Mr. Hecht was smiling now. "It's going to be one good favor for Gabe . . . Gabriel who loved music."

The following evening at just about the time the twilight hour slips like a soft shawl over the great stone shoulders of New York, a boy said a prayer in a cathedral. It was not an unusual prayer. It was simple, direct, and full of the intimacies of human language. It was the prayer of a boy who had learned all his life to talk quietly to God.

The Foundling

Peter Lane was waiting and smiling in the Lady Chapel.

"You see . . . I have a future now, God. Something really to bank on . . . something I've been wanting all my life . . . Thirty-five dollars a week . . . steady job with a future . . . chance for advancement. And a musical education on the side . . . I needed it, God . . . You know it . . . You know everything . . . And it's wonderful, the things that can happen to you inside twenty-four hours . . . the new hopes and dreams you can get . . . the people you meet . . . the faces you had never seen before . . . Mr. Hecht, for instance . . . Yes, especially the people, God . . . That's why I came here tonight . . . mostly for that . . . to thank You for the people I've known . . . friends . . . all the friends who have helped me, loved me . . . Thanks for these people . . . and please, God, help me to pay back everything . . . some day."

A man with one arm was standing off in the shadow of the High Altar of the Cathedral.

"Let's go, Paul," Peter whispered.

"Okay."

As they were passing the Pieta, Paul Taggart hesitated. He was studying the Madonna.

"In Hebrew, her name is Miriam, Paul." Peter said.

"Miriam?"

"Yes."

"It's a beautiful name, Peter."

"And she's a beautiful Madonna."

"Yes." Paul's voice was husky. "Yes, I'm getting to know that."

The Foundling

Outside the cathedral, Paul Taggart touched Peter's shoulder. "Know what time it is?"

"I haven't the slightest idea."

"It's June."

Peter laughed. "And I told Barbara I'd bring her a present with strings, in June."

"Will you promise me something, Peter?"

"Sure."

"Will you make good on finishing that symphony?"

"Well, I . . ."

"You can do it."

"Okay, Paul. I'll finish it . . . some day."

"It's a promise?"

"Yes."

"A promise right here on the steps of the cathedral?"

"That's right."

"Okay. And now something else . . ." Paul began to smile broadly. "Dig down into your pocket and get set to spend some money, Mr. Lane."

"What for?"

"For a present wrapped in strings."

Peter was puzzled for a moment.

"You're a big money-man now, thanks to Snoggins Mulrooney and Mr. Hecht."

Peter laughed. "That's right. Monday morning I start learning how to run a department store."

"What a career man! From cows and groceries to symphonies and suits!"

"That's right, Paul, suits and then suites!"

The Foundling

Their laughing scared dozens of pigeons off the cathedral steps.

"Now listen to me, Peter."

"I'm listening."

"Buy Barbara a present wrapped in strings. Buy yourself a ticket to Boston. Go to Lynnford. Propose to the girl. Marry her. And then live happily ever after."

"Paul," Peter gripped Taggart by the arm. "You're a grand guy."

"You're telling me? But hurry up. June's almost over."

Chapter 25

PETER HAD it planned perfectly. He would propose to Barbara out by Bodiou's farm. That was the place! So, by long distance telephone, Peter announced his sudden visit to the Ross family. By train, he arrived in Boston. And by bus, he landed at the elm-lined street in Lynnford. He had the present wrapped in strings and tucked in his pocket. Pearls. Forty-dollar pearls!

"Peter!" It was the happy voice of Mrs. Ross. Her arms were around him. She would make a swell mother-in-law, Peter thought.

"Glad to see you, Peter!" Mr. Ross greeted him. Peter was sure Mr. Ross would make the grandest kind of father-in-law.

"Hi, Peter!" Young Jackie Ross, together with Peter's other prospective brothers-in-law, gathered around him.

But where was Barbara, his future wife?

"Barb's upstairs, Peter."

"Oh," Peter sighed in relief.

"How long are you staying, Peter?" Jackie asked.

"I've got to get back to New York by Monday."

"So soon?" Mrs. Ross asked.

"I've got a big job waiting for me, Mrs. Ross." Peter announced with just the right amount of emphasis, since there was nothing like letting your in-laws know how financially sound you were. (Thank God for Mr. Hecht. Oh, thank you, God, for Mr. Hecht. Oh, thank you, Paul and Snoggins!)

"Why, hello, Noodles!"

Peter's pulse quickened at the sound of Barbara's voice. She descended the stairs slowly in a bright print dress. "This really is a surprise," she said, holding out her hand.

For some vague reason, Peter was troubled. Barbara seemed to be different, a creature of new poise and grace, almost cool. She wasn't a bit excited. Your future wife should get excited, Peter reasoned.

Later that afternoon, Peter started his campaign in a roundabout way. "How about taking a walk this evening, Barb?"

"Where?"

"Somewhere," he said, mysteriously. The pearls burned in his coat pocket.

"Somewhere?"

"Out around an old familiar spot, Barbara."

Barbara's eyebrows lifted in curiosity. She was remarkably mature and cool, Peter thought uncomfortably.

"We'll have to be back in time for Uncle Jim and Aunt Sue," Barbara cautioned.

"Uncle Jim and Aunt . . .?"

"They're coming here this evening, Peter."

Peter felt he was losing control of the situation. Uncle Jim and Aunt Sue! Just ordinary relations! Who were they compared to him, Peter Lane, willing to walk beyond all curfews to the ends of the earth with Barbara?

"We'll be back early," he said sourly.

"Uncle Jim is a dear."

Uncle Jim!

"Will you go, Barb?"

"Certainly, I'll go."

The familiar road to Bodiou's was less ethereal than Peter had dreamed. Burned patches of grass blackened the banks, and the yellowing honeysuckle vines along the stone walls had long lost their fragrance. Even the sky looked dark.

"We might be in for some rain, Peter," Barbara said.

"You don't mind rain, Barb."

"How far are we going?"

"Out to an old spot," Peter repeated. "Don't you want to go?"

"Well . . ." She was studying the sky with a degree of speculation that Peter found disconcerting.

Maybe Barbara didn't love him. Maybe she was just bored with this walk. And this was the evening he was going to propose!

There was an awkward silence when they reached the old pasture fence. This was the proper and sentimental spot Peter had chosen. It was here she had stood beside him long ago with her braids dangling perkily over her shoulders. It was most appropriately here that he should now look into her eyes and tell her how much he wanted her for a wife. He wasn't going to ask her in a burst of boyish fervor. He was a man now. He had a future, thanks to Mr. Hecht. There was no sense in getting excited.

But Peter, in spite of everything he said to himself, was fearfully and tremblingly excited.

"Well, here we are," Barbara said.

Peter's heart was thumping in his throat. "Yes, here we are."

The clouds to the west were piling up into smoke-gray mountains, and the red dance of lightning leaped distantly in the haze. Far back of the hills, thunder tumbled in slow booms and then leveled off like a muffled growl in the throat of a beast.

"Looks bad out there," Barbara said.

"Just another storm."

"We'd better not stay too long, Peter."

The lightning flickered again. Mother Nature who had, up to now, provided little in the way of proper romantic atmosphere was certainly rubbing it in.

"Barbara."

"Yes?"

"I wrote to you many times about a present I was going to bring you . . . wrapped in strings. Remember?"

"Yes."

"Well, I've got it for you."

"Peter, I didn't want you to bring me . . ."

"This is not what I planned on giving you," he confessed, taking the box out of his pocket and giving it to her. "There was something else I had in mind, but it . . . well, it didn't work out the way I wanted it to."

When Barbara lifted the pearls out of the box, her eyes were dancing. "Why, Peter, they're beautiful!"

"Here. I'll put them on you," he said, still trembling.

This was the moment! His heart would come tumbling out now in a long, fervent plea. Even while he snapped the clasp behind her neck, he would speak to her over her shoulder. Purple skies or no purple skies, there was nothing in all creation that could stem the tide of his speaking his longing for her.

"Barbara," Peter choked. The clasp was exasperatingly small between his fingers and it slipped twice.

"Yes, Peter?"

"Barbara, I wanted to tell you . . ."

She faced him then, and her white fingers caressed the string of pearls. "They're so lovely, Peter!" She stood there with her dark hair blowing slightly in the gust of the coming storm. She was beautiful.

"Barbara, I wanted to tell you that . . . that . . ." Peter was breathless. It was fear, plain and simple. Not the fear of framing an age-old question. That would have been easy enough. Rather, it was the fear of seeing Barbara's eyes caught suddenly with surprise and sympathy and refusal. She might laugh at him; she might even return the pearls with regret.

The Foundling

"Barbara, I wanted to say . . ."

"Yes, Peter?"

"I wanted to say . . . I hope you like the pearls . . . and . . . well, it was the least I could do."

Barbara's face was puzzled.

"I mean . . . you were always kind to me, Barb . . . and . . . well, a girl like you deserves pearls."

"Why, thank you, Peter."

"And now, maybe we ought to start home. The rain's coming on fast."

Then it happened!

As he turned to leave, Barbara's face was lifted to him. The dark intensity of her eyes, almost petulant, almost hurt, like the eyes of a child who had been refused something, caught Peter by surprise.

"Coming, Barbara?"

Her fingers were tight on his sleeve, and her mouth was trembling.

"What's the matter, Barb?"

"Why did you bring me these pearls?" she asked, and her eyes were black and smouldering.

"It was just a gift, Barbara, and I wanted to . . . to give you a present."

The tears came in a quick rush to her eyes. "You don't love me, Peter Lane. You never loved me. You just bring presents and write nice letters." Her voice was sobbing. "You're just trying to be nice to me."

"But Barbara . . ."

"Not once did you ever tell me you loved me. You'll go

The Foundling

back to New York, and then you'll . . . you'll . . ." She was crying in earnest then.

The rain was already on her face when Peter reached out and swept her into his arms.

That evening, Peter proposed to Barbara over a glass of limeade in Mowgler's grocery store. They were sitting at the new ice cream counter Mr. Mowgler had installed. Barbara was like a small girl, clutching his hand on the high seat. Her face and hair were tinted beautifully under the green neon sign.

"We've been sitting here for a whole hour, Peter," she said.

"I want to sit here for days, Barb. I just want to sit here and listen to you say it over and over again. You'll be my wife?"

"Yes."

"Forever and forever?"

"Forever and ever, Peter."

That was all that mattered. Immediately outside there was a world teeming with ominous phases and incidents: National Selective Service Act, fifty thousand men playing war games in the valleys of Tennessee, Churchill warning the House of Commons of danger in the Mediterranean, loggers striking in Puget Sound, machinists walking out in San Francisco, bombs in London, tanks in France . . . But all this was far, far away from Peter and Barbara tonight.

"Forever and forever, Barbara?"

"Forever and ever, Peter."

PART 5

Chapter 26

LETTER August 17, 1941

"..... *Paul Taggart and Ellen were standing in the room watching when I was sworn in with the rest of the fellows. There must have been about two hundred people there, relatives of the fellows, who crowded into the room* . . .

"*I'm on the train now, Barbara, and if this letter looks a bit bumpy, you'll know the reason. We go into quarantine as soon as we get to camp. After that it will be a snap* . . .

"*Sister Margaret gave me a leather bound diary, so when I come back I'll have plenty to read* . . ."

DIARY September 10, 1941

"..... *Must have gone five miles in the truck to the firing range. No practice scheduled. Major Wade lectured on heavy artillery. We discover he has a temper. Almost blew the roof when he learned Benny Lieber was imitating a woodpecker throughout lecture* . . ."

The Foundling

DIARY October 14, 1941

"..... *Letter from Barbara today. Am thinking about joining paratroops. Went down to field and watched planes circle jumping strip. They threw out colored dummy chutes first, evidently to test wind. Next trip around, the planes dumped the fellows. Must have been about twenty of them. Thought I could hear the silk snap in the wind when chutes opened. All the fellows yelled to each other as they floated down. Wonder what it would be like to jump . . ."*

DIARY November 1, 1941

"..... *Letter from Sister Margaret. Says she's knitting sweater for me. Found out Sergeant Harris hasn't been to church in years. Laughed at me when I asked him to go to Mass this morning. I'm going to keep after him . . ."*

DIARY December 2, 1941

"..... *Billy Colgan and myself on K.P. Also Lieber. Tommy Lieber is from Brooklyn, and he imitates Tommy Riggs and Betty Lou (Suzy Boo). Even Harris laughs at Lieber, and that's something. Major Wade boiling mad for some reason tonight—possibly because of gun parts left uncovered, range 62. We'll hear about it in the morning. Tonight, however, everybody's talking about a Christmas furlough. Hope we get it . . ."*

LETTER December 8, 1941

"..... *The news broke like wildfire over the camp. Even the air seemed different. It was as if that explosion at Pearl Harbor sent a shudder into the earth. Up to now, I'll admit*

The Foundling

I wasn't interested in this one year stretch. I wanted to get it over with and go home. Most of the fellows felt that way too. But it's different now, Barbara. I don't want to come back until this business is done. It took something like this attack at Pearl Harbor to make me realize how much I love these old United States. I mean it, Barbara. It's more than a map to me now. It's like something that's wounded and crying somewhere out there in the Pacific.

"Chaplain Cotter spoke at the Mass this morning. He told us he had prepared a sermon on Mary as our Mother as well as the Mother of God, but with the declaration of war only minutes away, he felt it was necessary to remind us of the heavy obligations we were about to undertake. I'll always remember the way he closed the sermon. He told us that America has been dedicated to Our Blessed Mother, and that if our country was being forced to declare war on her feast day, Mary would see us through. And I'm sure she will, Barbara . . ."

LETTER December 28, 1941

". . . . . Thanks for the sweater you sent, Sister Margaret. It fits me like a glove. Knowing that you knit it yourself, I'm sure it will be as good as any bullet-proof jacket the army can provide. No. I'm not joining the paratroopers. I have decided to stick with the infantry. So you can stop having those nightmares about parachutes that don't open.

"Did I tell you that I got a letter from Mr. Mulrooney? He says if the war doesn't end soon, he's going to volunteer himself. Mr. Hecht also wrote. I'm going to get a letter off

The Foundling

to him tonight. I owe that man plenty, Sister. More than I can tell you.

"According to the latest reports we may be moving within the next two weeks. Nobody knows where we are going.

"The fellows standing next to me in the pictures are Ed Galvin and Tom Lieber. Lieber comes from Brooklyn and some of these days I'm going to bring him to see you. He'll have all the Sisters laughing when they hear Suzy Boo. Suzy is a little four year old voice he uses."

LETTER December 28, 1941

". . . . . *Chaplain Cotter asked me to play the organ at Midnight Mass. It's a beautiful electric organ, Barbara, the first one I've ever played. The army supplies one for every chapel. If you could only have been down here and listened to the way the fellows sang 'Silent Night, Holy Night.' It was something I won't forget for a long time. I can see them coming into the chapel again—Billy Colgan, Major Wade, and Louise, the colored girl from Fayetteville, with her box of starched shirts for Lieutenant Rodriguez. I remember these three particularly because they were standing around the organ before Mass began.*

"*It was a good night, Barbara, for even rough and tumble Major Wade had some mist in his eyes when he turned the pages for me on the organ rack and bellowed with all the sincerity of his heart, 'Round yon virgin mother and child, holy infant so tender and mild.' And Louise, in her husky alto sang a nice harmony in thirds to the Major. Everybody was longing for home that night. Not that tears or sentiment* are everything, Barbara, but I couldn't help thinking that the world would never be at war if all men could gather around a crib again. This may sound strange to you, but I think that even Major Wade would have made room for a Jap or a German that night. I'm sure he would, Barbara. We weren't soldiers that night. We weren't officers or buck privates, white or black. We were simply people trying to remember that Christ came to earth for all men.

"Hope you got the present I sent.

"I love you more than ever. Love me because I need you more and more . . ."

LETTER January 22, 1942

". . . . . Los Angeles is a long way from that stairway to track 12 at the Penn Station, Barb. I didn't dream that we'd be moving out so quickly but that makes little difference now. That last afternoon we had together in New York is something I keep remembering. It wasn't what you said to me that afternoon that matters so much now. It was the way you looked at me, Barbara, when I asked you if you would get tired waiting for me. You didn't answer—not with words, Barb. But when you threw your arms around me outside track 12 I didn't need words. I can't help loving you the way I do. And I can't forget the way you looked at me when I went through the gates. I've seen that look in the faces of so many women outside train gates. And every woman I've seen was you. I guess I've never stopped seeing you, the eyes and nose and lips of you. I saw your face clearly and definitely in the frame of the window as we

The Foundling

rattled through Trenton, Philadelphia, Baltimore, Washington and points south. I saw your face smiling at me in the fog outside St. Louis, and across the flat plains of Texas. You were very near to me in the orange burst of the sunrise I saw coming up over the valleys of California yesterday. Barbara, we're going farther away from each other all the time, and I don't know how things will turn out. It's just that I want to keep saying over and over again that I love you . . . You're the best and dearest thing God ever gave me. I wish you were here. Please never stop loving me . . ."

LETTER February 18, 1942
". . . Even with V mail I can't tell you where I am, Mr. Mulrooney. But I can tell you that I've been getting a lot of callouses on my hands along a waterfront. We must have loaded at least a hundred tons of wool this afternoon, and that's no exaggeration. I think I'd rather be a sacristan right now. Oh, for the good old Bronx!"

LETTER March 3, 1942
". . . . . Lieber, that fellow I was telling you about, kept the gang in good spirits, Paul. You really need a sense of humor in this army, and Lieber's got it. Suzy Boo, that's the voice of a little girl Lieber imitates, this Suzy Boo stuff, had all the civilians on the dock holding their sides when Lieber was loading with the fellows. Got eight letters in a batch from Barbara. Heard from Mr. Mulrooney. Signs himself Snoggins. Also heard from Chub Sands. He's somewhere in Europe, and he still remembers that suit you gave him a long

time ago. He spoke about it in his last letter . . . Keep smiling. Love to Ellen . . ."

LETTER March 27, 1942
". . . . . We've been doing a lot of field maneuvers for the past week, following up with night tactics. But it would bore you, Barb, so let's skip it. Anyway, I'd rather talk about us.

"You're such a honey to do what you've done. And it was swell of your mother and father to let you go to New York to visit my 'family.' Thanks! How thrilled Ellen and Paul must be to have you! They are my family, you know. They're all the family I've ever had. Ellen is swell, isn't she? Paul's been more to me than I can ever tell you.

"I love the snapshot of Ellen and you in your Nurse's Aid uniform. I'm so glad you're with my 'family' for a while. Visit them as often as you can, won't you?

"You'll probably think this is silly, but do you know there were days, especially on the ocean, when I worried. A girl can't marry a fellow on love alone. A man should have enough to start a home with. He needs a decent job. That worried me a lot. I owe much to Mr. Hecht even though I never really started working for him. My number was drawn too quickly out of that bowl. But as far as my future goes, listen to this. It's about Billy Colgan.

"One afternoon Billy Colgan and I got talking. He's like a kid but he's really swell. Anyway, Barbara, that afternoon he took a picture out of his wallet—a snapshot of a young girl standing on a lawn. 'That's my wife,' he said. It was the first time I knew that Colgan was married. They're going

The Foundling

to have a baby and he's on top of the world. Colgan is the kind of fellow who married on a shoe string. He had a small job with a wire company in New York before he married. He didn't have too much to look forward to, but at least he had a small hold on life.

"Colgan, with that creased picture of his wife in his wallet, made me stop worrying. He did more to encourage me than any sermon I've ever listened to. That's the truth. The more I thought about it, the more I realize how genuine a fellow like Colgan is. His whole attitude, the way he spoke, the light in his eyes, he's swell.

"The more I thought about it, the more I knew that's all I'll need. Just a shoestring hold on life. We'll be able to make a go of it. If I never get back with Mr. Hecht (but he said he'd take me back), what would you think about a place in the Adirondacks, perhaps? I was a farmer, once. Remember? We could always be together. December, January, February and all the months. We could ship cream and milk on the morning trains to New York. And I'd be able to write that fourth movement I was telling you about. It's been unfinished business for too long. But somehow I feel tonight I'll be able to do it. Then I'll buy you a real beaver coat, sheared or shirred, however you spell it. But it will be a good coat.

"And when Sister Crescentia's symphony is finished, we'll all go to Carnegie Hall to hear it. Paul and Ellen and Sister Margaret, Mr. Mulrooney, Mr. Hecht, Chubby, Billy Colgan and his wife. They'll all be there. And we'll all go to Gallagher's for a six inch steak . . .

"Oh, Barbara, life is going to be good for us, I hope and pray . . ."

LETTER April 10, 1942

". . . . . It's perfectly awful, Chub, how friends can live in the same city and only see each other a few times. It's particularly true of New York and I have been regretting now that we didn't get together more when we could. When this mess is over, we won't let it happen again.

"Thanks for your letter. I was sorry, but in a way glad, to hear about poor Jean. But it was a good way to go— singing happily in old Sam Cooper's flat and then the quick heart attack and dying in his arms with you and Noella standing by. Bless her, and may God take care of her soul.

"It's nice to hear you have been entertaining your buddies with your music when you could. I've been doing the same here. Mark Ross would be delighted to know that I have learned to play pieces that will please him. I must remember to tell Barbara.

"Sister Margaret knitted me a sweater and I have been receiving dozens of letters from Paul and Ellen and my Barbara. Boy, what those letters mean! There's one poor kid here who only gets one about every month and he's the most miserable guy you ever saw.

"I hope every thing's going all right at home for you. I was so proud when you told me that you had become half owner of that stationery store. Having the customers come to you to buy their newspapers instead of your hawking them in the streets. That's all right. When the war's over, I expect you to own a whole chain of them.

"And having Noella work in the store instead of cleaning those old floors—that's all right, too. Be sure to give her my love when you write to her.

"Well, so long, Chub, take care of yourself . . ."

DIARY September 18, 1942

". . . . . Brisbane is fading off the stern. We're moving into the theater of operations. Theater is a funny word for it. I'm going to save these notes. Someday, they'll print me up in a full section of the Evening Journal.

"Sergeant Harris is parading the deck like a Commodore. He went to Confession last night for the first time in years. He's a good skate. He gave me a comb with a little snapper clasp on it—sort of a fountain pen clasp that can catch the fold of your pants pocket. But what'll I do with a comb when I get to wherever I'm going?"

DIARY September 27, 1942

". . . . . Land sighted off starboard. It's Port Moresby, New Guinea."

DIARY October 8, 1942

". . . . . Same stuff. Still moving along the coast. The rain keeps coming, and my shoes are really soft now. Captain Rowan is getting more friendly. He's even talking to Hughie Lynn who could have been court martialed for the language he used against the 126th, Harris, and the U.S. Army. But you can't blame Lynn. Some of the fellows are throwing up their food, and you can't hike ten hours on a sick stomach . . . Japs are somewhere ahead."

DIARY October 12, 1942
". . . . . We've got a two-hour breather, and I'm sitting on the ground against a tree. Just got to thinking as my heels dug through the earth that it's really the same earth that I've always known. A man couldn't find much difference in it, except for the mineral elements that would make it different for some expert in a laboratory. And the sky above me is the same blue. Even the atmosphere is familiar. I've had this same tropical feeling in sections of the Bronx Botanical Gardens. The chatter of these jungle birds reminds me of thick bags of peanuts bought outside the zoo. The world isn't very different or strange. The world at this moment in New Guinea is familiar and kind. Why couldn't all men be familiar and kind too?"

DIARY October 15, 1942
". . . . . We must have covered more than sixty miles along the coast out of Moresby. Reports say Japs are in vicinity. Colgan didn't make it to Company."

DIARY October 18, 1942
". . . . . It's raining again and we're waiting for move out signal from Rowan. Jap scouts contacted. It looks as if we'll be running into them soon. Plane dropped supplies one hour after two Mitzies circled over us. Not on patrol either. Mitzies don't patrol. Johnson spotted them from the beach and we scrambled fast."

The Foundling

DIARY October 22, 1942

". . . . . Colgan still tired. Can't keep up with Company. Afraid, he'll get pinked with delay snipers . . . Tired. Company running out of supplies."

DIARY October 28, 1942

". . . . . Wonder if we'll make Owen Stanley Mts. Far north. Am tired but too nervous to sleep. Seven hours through jungle. Plenty of Halzone pills in water. I keep thinking of a funeral coach at Mount Mary. Must have been that field day. I'm nutty. Tired. Two quinines yesterday. Four today. Still no Japs."

DIARY November 2, 1942

". . . . . Jungle steaming with heat. Gets me in forehead where sweat stings. Company mostly tired and thirsty. But Tommy has fellows laughing with Suzy Boo in fox hole. Suzy wants Tommy to go home. Japs waiting two or three miles ahead. Hope I can keep going."

DIARY November 5, 1942

". . . . . First casualties . . . Lost two men last night. Barbier got stomach wound. We lay six or seven hours in river bed. Rowan sprained ankle but still with us. He's a good fellow. Personally led run that cleared snipers off bank this morning. Up Sligo, he roared. Didn't know he was an Irishman."

DIARY November 8, 1942

". . . . . We're in deep now. Still moving to Stanley Mts. Thirsty and drank rain off hat. Love to have a coke right

The Foundling

now. Colgan is smiling. He wonders if it's a boy or a girl, because his baby is expected to arrive in November."

DIARY November 10, 1942

". . . . . Taking eight quinines daily. Dysentery is spreading. Heat must be 110. Patrols report Japs closing in. We may meet them tonight. Out of supplies. Jesus, Mary and Joseph help us."

DIARY November 11, 1942

". . . . . Captain Ed. Rowan killed with shell fragment. We lost four other men last night—one insane . . . got up and ran into swamp."

DIARY November 12, 1942

". . . . . More Japs coming up. Harris says we move across tonight. This may be last entry. Wonder if I'll come out alive. I think I'm ready for tonight."

DIARY November 18, 1942

". . . . . Bogged down. Lay in swamp all night. Bombing and shelling around us. Still waiting for Harris to give the word . . ."

Chapter 27

THE Corporal explained it in this manner:

"We were holding a position two hundred, maybe two hundred and fifty yards in front of the forward snipe fire of the enemy. We advanced another sixty yards and then lay low. We waited fifteen, maybe twenty minutes. I was next to Lane. I said to him, 'We move in two minutes, Lane. Artillery is coming up fast.' He said, 'All right.' I said, 'Do you hear me, Lane? We move in two minutes.' I repeated it because he looked kind of dopey to me. Glassy-eyes, sort of . . .

"Well, anyway, that's how it was before we moved. The artillery opened up behind us, and that was the signal. Lane jumps to his feet and starts running. All of us ran. We covered about seventy, maybe eighty yards. It was easy. Our forward scouts were laughing. They said it was all cleaned out up ahead. So we kept moving.

The Foundling

"Then it happened. About twenty feet to the left of us, we see Lane lying on his face. He was hit hard by a snipe bullet. 'They got Lane' Lieber yells. But the C.O. yells louder, 'Lay low. They're still ahead.' But Lieber didn't hear. The C.O. screams and curses at Lieber. 'Get down—' the C.O. yells. Lieber takes cover.

"Then everything was sort of a quick jumble. It was like this. Lane, who's wounded, is lying out there and he's groaning. He's in an open clearing. He was trying to crawl back when all of a sudden a hand grenade lands two feet away from him. It doesn't explode yet. It just rolls and stops near Lane. The grenade lands two feet from Lane, who is practically knocked out. Then Lieber jumps up and starts running towards Colgan. He says only two words while he is running. 'O God!' It was like a scream and a prayer . . . Then he ran to where the hand grenade was, right next to Lane. He lifts it up quick, and is just about to throw it away, when—bang. You guessed it. Right off in his face. The last I see of Lieber is, he's falling backwards. The guy is killed instantly. Lane gets hit with the same grenade. And then everything went quiet. That's my report, sir."

(B.M.S.—Pfc.)

Chapter 28

MAJOR ERWING, the staff surgeon, was cheerful that night. "You'll be up and around in a few weeks, Lane."

"How about my eyes, Major? When does the bandage come off?"

"Soon."

He was walking away when Peter called after him.

"Yes, Lane. What can I do for you?"

"Please tell me, sir. What's wrong with my eyes?"

The Major ran his fingers lightly over the bandage on Peter's head. "You really want to know, Lane?"

"Yes."

Major Erwing sighed. Then he spoke slowly, like a man in a reverie. "Once upon a time, there were many fellows lying in a dark room. They were puzzled, Lane. Some of them were frightened. And they always asked an old Major about it. 'What's wrong with my eyes, Major?' That's the question they always asked. Every one of them. And the Major would answer, 'There's nothing wrong with your eyes, fellows. There's nothing wrong with the eyes a man has given for the defense of his country.' That's what the old Major always said, Lane."

The Major walked away.

Everything was now wholly black for Peter Lane. His fingers were twisting in the sheets. He was sobbing, "It's a blackout. It's a blackout, Barbara."

Then black became blacker for Peter Lane. Darkness descended upon darkness, over him, around him.

A soldier's voice was speaking from the next bed. "At least you're alive, buddy."

Alive!

Peter nodded slowly. He could not say anything. There was nothing to say. But somewhere, in some far corner of this darkness, a pin-point of light was suddenly stirring. And because he remembered a very foolish thing, the voice of a small girl, Suzy Boo, Peter Lane cried and said, "Tommy Lieber."

"Yeah, at least you're alive," the soldier's voice repeated.

"He used to make them laugh along the docks in Australia," Peter said.

"What did you say, buddy?"

"Nothing."

"Oh?"

"It wasn't anything at all."

"Good night, buddy."

"Good night."

Chapter 29

IT WAS Spring, 1943.

It was a sunny day at Pearl Harbor and Chaplain Cummings seemed buoyantly happy. "You spoke very well at the Mass, your Excellency," Chaplain Cummings said.

His Excellency, grateful for this bit of clerical fidelity, might have been tempted to recommend that this enthusiastic admirer be named a Monsignor were it not for the fact that most priests at some time or another have told their Bishops they spoke well.

Chaplain Cummings was folding the altar linens in the kit when he continued. "By the way, there's a boy here whom I'd like you to see if you could spare the time."

The Bishop consulted his watch. "I plan to call on the General, but first I shall be glad to see this boy of yours."

"Only five minutes of your time, your Excellency. I know this fellow would appreciate it."

They found the soldier sitting alone. Smoked glasses shielded his eyes, and when the Chaplain introduced him to the Bishop, he rose quickly.

"Peter Lane, your Excellency. He's one of your own boys."

The Bishop was startled when he heard the name. "Are you Peter Lane from Mount Mary?"

"Yes, Bishop. I met you back there on two of your visits."

They sat there for over two hours. As the Bishop listened to the story of the boy's life unfold, he knew again and forever the tragedy of war. This was not a glib interview for the magazines and journals. It was not the tabulated exploits of the veteran, recorded in the genial setting of canteens, brass bands, and photographers' bulbs. It was, rather, the after-hour story, the hesitant but sure revelation of scars that had been cauterized and bandaged every day against public probing. It was the conqueror, the G.I. campaigner reduced to a boy, lonely and afraid.

Peter's lips were forming the words in even, calculating phrases. "I think I can take it, now that the doctors have told me the worst. But sometimes, Bishop, I get frightened."

"What seems to be the trouble?"

"It's myself. It's the doubts that keep pressing on me." His voice cracked with utter weariness. "It's everything."

The Bishop weighed the boy's mood. It was a tremor of suppressed pain spoken from a hospital chair. By all the proprieties of his priesthood, the Bishop was expected to formulate a soothing sentence, spiritually cogent and com-

The Foundling

forting. Instead, he dallied momentarily with an uncertain dread that was in his own thinking. He said, "You haven't been fighting the war in vain, Peter."

"That's what I keep trying to tell myself. Maybe it's true. But it's not the war I'm worrying about. It's something worse than war."

"And what is that, Peter?"

The blind soldier tapped the cane against his shoe and a cold monotony was in his voice. "I guess it's . . . maybe it's the fear of losing my faith in life, in living."

"You're not serious, Peter."

"Bishop," he was like a small boy now, and his hand trembled when he pushed his fingers through his hair, "Bishop, you'll never know what it's like to have everything get black around you. It's not only losing your eyes. It's even worse than the screams and the ether and the sirens. It's just . . . it's the awful loneliness in a world that's getting too saturated with hate."

"You're tired and strained, Peter."

"I can't stop thinking about it. I was just another one of millions of other fellows trying to get a little happiness out of life. I wanted Barbara and a home. I wanted to settle down and live and have kids. I've got only one life to live, and I want to live it in peace, but there isn't any peace. All you need is one ear to hear it. I could've written back home about it . . . could've told them a lot of things about this war and the fellows in it. I'm not a pessimist. I'm only trying to call things as I see them. And I can tell you there's been a lot of hatred and suspicions all along, a lot of filth and greed, and too much noise, noise. They're even laying two to one that we'll be back in it again with Russia inside of a couple of years."

This was the undercurrent, the seething tide of discontent spoken in the bitter words of a soldier. The Bishop, of course, adhering to traditional patriotic optimism, would return home and speak of glowing deeds done on the battle-fronts. He would write speeches in the bright vein of national hopes, of international fusions of good will and preparations for lasting peace. The Bishop, under a compelling ritual demanding profound and patriotic sentiment, would search his concordance and his dictionary for the appropriate message to the American mothers, fathers, sweethearts; he would stand again at a tomb in Arlington; he would submit to a hundred polite invitations to canonize the war effort, and the victory, and the peace. It was a vocation, being a Bishop; one raised a shepherd's staff above one's troubled flock and pointed to pastures made secure on the green slopes of the New World Brotherhood.

But where was the Brotherhood? Where were the green slopes? Where and what were the words that could shut out from the ears of a blind boy the noises of the new hates, the endless contentions of capital and labor back home, the pounding of innumerable court gavels at the foundations of the family, the sneer and snarl at race and religion? What and where were the words that could drown the ears of a blind boy to the incoherent mumbling of the sick, the diseased, the starving lying prostrate on all the bloodied roads that run in the wake of war? What words

The Foundling

could soothe the crying of human despair in a night seared with flame and the screams of loved ones burned in the holocaust of war?

The Bishop reached out and held the blind boy's arm. "Peter, I think I know what you mean. I, also, have reason to know the dreads and doubts of life." And because the Bishop was human, he shivered in his brief moment of introspection.

"Peter, I know what you mean," the Bishop said. "There's only one answer to all your doubts and dreads."

"What's the answer?"

"Faith, Peter. You know that. Faith and hope in Jesus Christ who taught us how to rise out of the rubble and ruin of this world's many calvaries. He knew what it was to have the light fade from His eyes. He knew what it was to be a lonely soldier."

Peter cupped his blind eyes in his fingers. His voice was penitent, quiet. "Yes. I guess I knew the answer . . . knew it all the while. I only wanted to hear it again." He was breathing with difficulty. "It's something you just got to hear again and again, especially when all the lights have gone out."

"You were afraid."

"That's right. Afraid of myself, afraid that I'd never be happy again. You see, Bishop, a fellow banks a lot on happiness. He banks mostly on the girl he loves."

"Barbara is banking on you, too, Peter. She's waiting for you, Peter. She wants you home."

The boy's face was smiling now.

The Foundling

"Why don't you go home and give Barbara a chance, Peter?" the Bishop asked.

"I wonder what it's going to be like facing her?"

"You could even finish that symphony you told me about."

"I want to do that, too."

"When are you leaving for the States?"

"I don't know yet, Bishop. Chaplain Cummings asked me to stay on here as organist."

"I see. Will you remember to send me a telegram telling me when you'll arrive, Peter?"

The blind boy smiled. "I never sent a telegram to a Bishop."

The Bishop in that instant was acutely conscious of a frock coat, and a ring, and the dozen conventional and ecclesiastical niceties that had separated him from the simplicity of a day when children looked into his face and called him "Father."

"You'll send me a letter or a telegram, Peter? I'd rather a telegram."

"Yes, your Excellency."

On the following morning, the Bishop's plane lifted above the harbor and swung in a slow eastward arc. "Already I see the light of the Rising Sun," the Bishop read from the page of his breviary. Light, good, far-reaching light had risen and tipped the wings of the throbbing plane. The light was everywhere in the sky and on the water and all the world that morning seemed in the upslant of summer.

In reverie he thought of Australia's stalwart, red gum trees, reaching upwards as do all trees. And the grass on the plains beyond Adelaide, where uncounted flocks grazed with the crimson flush of dawn in their wool, it, too, was reaching upwards that morning. Northeastward, where the white pounding of the Pacific surf washed the small islands, a green, tropical world was lifting up tendrils and vines. Cherry trees were growing to the east and west and, oblivious to international dispute, proudly displayed their blossoms. Pandanus plants and coconut palms were reaching for the sun no differently from the yellow tulips in Holland or the lilacs and hollyhocks in the suburban gardens of New England.

All growing things were truly in the upslant of summer.

The Bishop shut his breviary, sat back in his seat and closed his eyes.

"Dear good God of all men, never let it be too late," he breathed. "Lift the hearts of all men in this rebirth of Thy creation. And Mary, mother of God, lift the heart of one boy who sits with smoked glasses on a beach so very far from home, and of all our boys who have borne the burden of war that our country might survive and be a beacon to the world, a living shrine of Liberty and Charity and Peace, and make all Americans worthy of our soldiers and of our soldiers' sacrifice."

Chapter 30

MARY, the portress who answers the door in a black dress and white apron, ushered them up the winding, red-carpeted stairway.

The man was tall and nervous.

"You're Mr. Taggart," the Bishop said.

"Yes, sir."

Mr. Taggart hesitated before he lifted his left hand.

"I'd be proud to shake your left hand, Mr. Taggart."

The grip of the man was powerful and warm.

"And you're Miss Ross, I believe."

"Yes, your Excellency." The girl kissed the ring on the Bishop's finger.

For a moment, they looked doubtful.

Miss Ross spoke first. "We received your telegram, your Excellency, and . . ."

"Yes. We're going to Mitchell Field immediately."

The Foundling

Miss Ross was puzzled. "Mitchell Field?"

"It's a surprise party," the Bishop continued. "Could you guess who might be coming in on a plane tonight?"

Both of them shouted the name in quick unison. "Peter!"

A few minutes later, they walked down the front steps of the graystone residence.

"Mitchell Field, Tom," the Bishop said to the big, genial chauffeur who was standing at the door of the limousine.

At twenty-two minutes past eleven, the plane, with its headlight pointing in a sharp downward beam on the runway, landed at the far end of the field.

"Twenty-two minutes late," the Bishop announced; but the man and girl standing beside him did not hear the words.

Barbara ran the twenty yards that separated her from the blind boy who was walking between two soldiers.

She was still crying in his arms, when Paul Taggart spoke. "Hello, Peter," he said quietly.

The boy lifted his face. "Paul!" he called in a choking voice.

It was wonderful and it was bewildering. While they chattered happily to him, a multitude of unrelated thoughts raced through his mind of Chubby; Chubby should be here, but of course he couldn't, he was still in Europe. *Please God, bring him home safe—and whole.* Mr. Hecht, well, Mr. Hecht wouldn't be here, he'd have to be at the store, but he would call on Mr. Hecht right away to tell him again how he had helped him in his darkest hour—well, and he smiled inwardly, his darkest hour up till that time. There was no pain or fear now, Barbara's kiss had erased that and he knew they

The Foundling

would be happy and, wasn't it strange? Paul must have felt the same way when first he went to Ellen with a scar on his face and an empty sleeve . . .

"Ellen," Paul echoed the name in his thoughts. "Ellen didn't know what the Bishop's message meant, so she didn't come, but I called her while we were waiting for your plane and she's expecting us, she's getting a home-coming supper ready . . . Bishop, I mean, your Excellency, could you . . .?"

But the Bishop smiled his reluctant inability to attend.

"And Mark," Barbara babbled on, "Mark and his wife will be in Lynnford for ten days, but they will be here for a couple of days. He said as soon as you got home he wanted you to play modern music for him, but I said no, we're through with that. The first thing we're going to work on is the Fourth Movement."

Oh, yes, Peter thought, *we,* we'll do that for Sister Crescentia and for us. You hear better when you're blind and so you'll compose better. This time Mr. Gerber will like it. And we'll play it for him as dear little Teresa used to play at the Mount. She was blind also and she was happy. I am blind, too, Peter thought, and I am being made happy . . .

"And Peter you must . . ." Paul said.

"And Peter, first thing . . ." Barbara said.

"And, friends," the Bishop interrupted good-naturedly, but with authority, "let's go now. You can say all this—and more—when you reach home!"

"Home." The word found echo in his pounding, joyous heart. He wanted to say so much, so very much. Instead, Bar-

The Foundling

bara spoke as she guided him to the car, "Imagine being met by a Bishop." And Peter whispered, "Imagine being met by *you*!"

The Bishop sat in the front seat with Tom. Once he looked backwards to see if everything was all right. The girl's head was resting quietly on the shoulder of the young, blind soldier.

"Yes," the Bishop concluded, "everything *is* all right."